STAYING STONED

High in the Mountains

RICHARD EBNER

Sketches by Glenn Foden and Richard Ebner

Staying Stoned
Copyright 2023 by Richard Ebner

All rights reserved.

This is a work of memoir. Great care has been taken regarding accuracy in portrayal of the incidents that are documented in this book. Any factual errors are the fault of the author and are not intentional.

ISBN: 978-1-958669-10-5

Printed in the United States

PROLOGUE

Staying Stoned was originally recorded on magnetic tape; no digital recording devices were available, no Google, no internet. As a result, the editing process was a nightmare. An excerpt near the end of the story expresses the editing problems better than I can in this prologue.

"Twelve hours of tape do not a book make. There is still all that typing someone must do and the editing. Oh God, the editing this mess of words will need, in order to make any sense, when someone tries to read it. All those run-on sentences will have to be chased down and stopped. The dangling participles can't be left dangling. Misplaced gerunds will have to be found and returned to their proper place. And the breaks in my speech, that might become excessive commas, could be a problem You see, this sort of tell-it-as-you-go story book is a real nightmare for an editor.

Of course, I could just transcribe it exactly as I said it. Sort of a James Joyce style stream of unconsciousness – my own portrait of myself as a young man," Theo wrote.

In 1978-79, when *Staying Stoned* was first recorded on magnetic tape, in addition to the editing problems, marijuana was illegal in all fifty states. The 'War on Drugs', as named by Richard Nixon, had already begun ten years earlier, and Nixon declared illegal drugs "Public Enemy Number One!" By 1982, Nancy Reagan was telling us to "Just say no."

All indications are that we have been spending billions of dollars a year on an unwinnable war. And just saying no hasn't worked out so well for many of us either.

Travel back in time as a 26-year-old carpenter attempts to reduce his personal harm, by taking a self-imposed sabbatical away from all of his addictive; substances, influencers, and environments.

For three months, starting on Christmas Day in 1978, Theo, and his Great Dane named Misty, hunkered down to attempt a drug free winter. At a summer camp, called Lime Kiln Camps, in the White Mountains of New Hampshire, the young man and his dog concentrated on staying warm, and on staying alive.

MOST OF THE NAMES HAVE BEEN CHANGED TO PROTECT THE GUILTY.

Before being named Lime Kiln Camp, it was called Black Mt. Camp – surveyor's map from 1959.

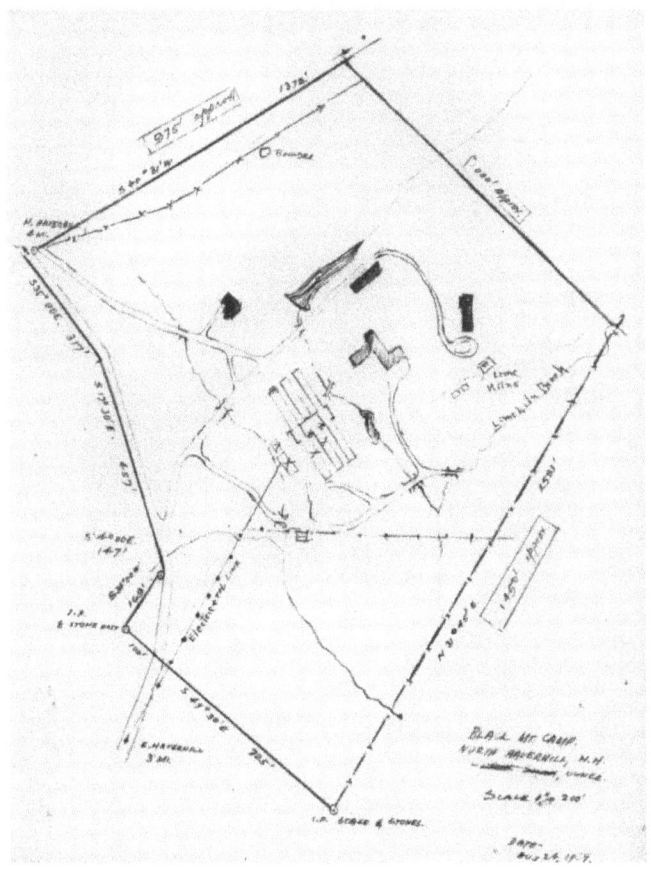

Lime Kiln Camp – Theo's map from 1978-79

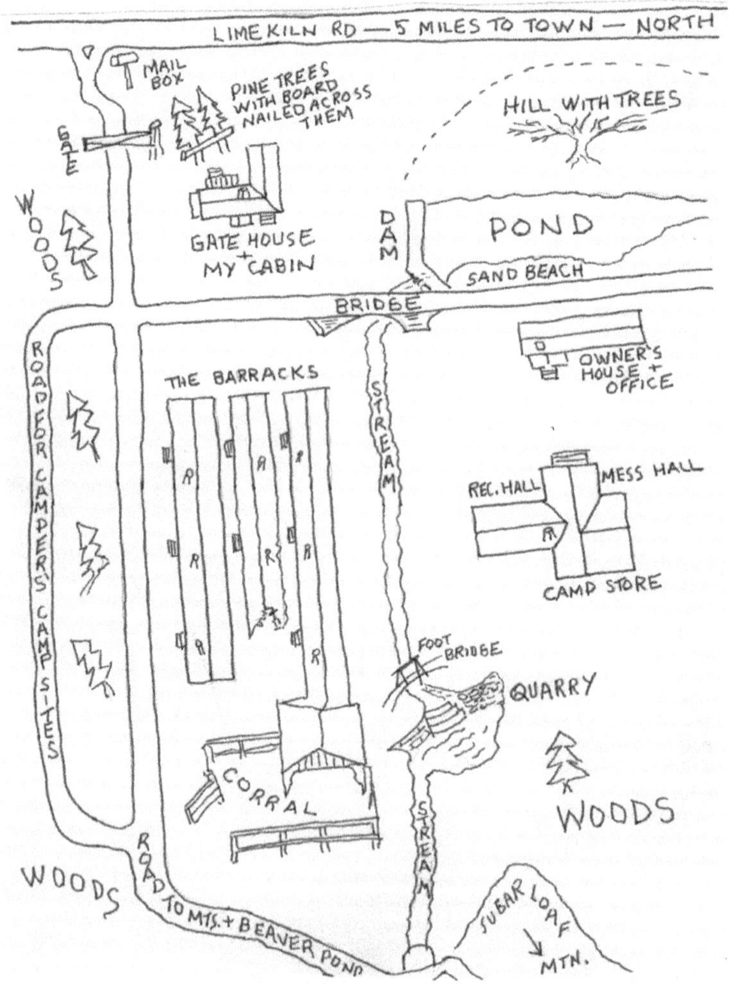

LIMEKILN RD — 5 MILES TO TOWN — NORTH
MAIL BOX
PINE TREES WITH BOARD NAILED ACROSS THEM
GATE
HILL WITH TREES
WOODS
GATE HOUSE + MY CABIN
DAM
POND
SAND BEACH
BRIDGE
ROAD FOR CAMPERS' CAMP SITES
THE BARRACKS
STREAM
OWNER'S HOUSE + OFFICE
REC. HALL
MESS HALL
CAMP STORE
FOOT BRIDGE
QUARRY
CORRAL
WOODS
STREAM
WOODS
ROAD TO MTS. + BEAVER POND
SUGAR LOAF MTN.

CHAPTER I

December, 25th 1978

Arrival
5:00 AM Monday, December 25, 1978

This is really weird man. I mean did you ever try to write a book, let alone record one on magnetic tape? I keep trying to think of something really heavy to start things off. You know, something spectacular to hold your interest. Something so fascinating that you can't possibly put this book down, so spellbinding that you don't even want to blink, lest your eyes might jump a line on the page and you would miss something. Even when you have a lot of interesting things to write about, as I do, expressing those thoughts isn't easy.

It is nice to know that someone is actually reading this

though. The idea of spending the next three months talking into this tape recorder and then typing it all down to create a book, is a bit overwhelming at the moment! If you hadn't come along and started reading this book, I could have gotten really depressed. So, let me say thanks.

When you were younger, did you ever wonder how the man on the radio knew that you were listening to his station? I did! The disc jockey would say, "You are listening to WPOT, Pot Rock 96." How the hell did he know? I could have had the TV on. Of course, now that we are older and much wiser, we know the trick. The guy just guessed that's all. No big deal, he guessed. So, that is how I knew you were reading this book.

It feels very strange to be sitting here on Christmas morning, in the cab of my pickup truck, miles away from home and all alone. The strangest thing is that no one is forcing me to do this and no one is paying me either. I don't know if that makes this whole book writing idea strange or if it just makes me dumb. I wasn't even stoned or tripping my brains out on acid when I thought of becoming a writer. Feeling a little weird for sure – but, I swear I was straight. So, what difference does it make, and who cares anyway, right?

Have you ever just let your mind wander while you were stoned, sometimes coming up with these really great ideas? Oh sure, sometimes you would have really stupid ideas and just think they were great. Like the time I thought of making an electric ice cream scooper. This scooper would heat up and melt the ice cream, making it easier to scoop out of the container. Pretty dumb huh? Seriously though, some of the ideas I have had while I was stoned have been quite profound and even earth shattering. Unfortunately, I can't remember any of them right now. One of the hazards of thinking while stoned I guess.

Speaking of ideas you get while you're high, there is something that really pisses me off. You have a great idea about how to make a lot of money. You say to yourself, this could actually work! You even start thinking about how to spend all the money you will be making. Then you forget about the idea for six months or so. One day, all of a sudden, you see your idea in a store or on TV and some jerk is making millions of dollars on your idea. There is a theory of mine, that there are these people who don't have any ideas of their own, but who can tune into other people's heads and steal their good ideas. Especially if you have an idea while you are stoned. That is why you can't remember it the next day.

I should tell you a little about what it is like here in the mountains. Limekiln Camp, where the cabin I will be staying in is located, is set at the base of two mountains – Sugarloaf and Black Mountain. The nearest big town is North Haverhill, NH, about five miles away down a dirt road. Entering the camp is like entering a secret hideout. Like the hole-in-the-wall-gang's hideout. The dirt road into it curves and dips, with woods very close on both sides. A gate with a sign appears in front of you:

WELCOME TO LIMEKILN CAMP—PLEASE CLOSE GATE.

Beyond the gate, the woods open up into a large field with several buildings and the mountains surrounding it all. Approximately twenty-five acres of land are part of the camp. Bordering it are thousands of acres of State and National Forest. The stone lime kiln in the drawing, stands near the Chippewa Trail close to Black Mountain in Haverhill, New Hampshire. It was originally built in 1842.

The Civilian Conservation Corps work program occupied

the site during the Depression, and repaired the kiln in 1941.

Back then, as many as three hundred men worked here year-round. These men worked in the quarry mining limestone, or at the kiln cooking the stone to get the lime from it. Of course, they needed housing for the workers, so they built several buildings called the barracks as well as the cabin I'll be staying in. Thanks, Glenn Foden, for the sketch.

Today this camp is privately owned, used for summer recreation, and is closed in the winter. Over the years, I have been coming here since I was still in my mother's womb, I have gotten to know the present owners quite well. They have been nice enough to let me stay here rent free, so that I can write for the winter.

Right now, I had better plow my way to my cabin, build a fire in the wood stove, and shut my truck off before it runs out of gas. Oh, I didn't tell you, there is a snow plow on the front of my truck and a blizzard raging outside. Details, details! It is going to be a White Christmas.

Did you ever spend Christmas completely alone? This will be the first time for me. Of course, I won't be completely alone, there is Misty, this tape recorder and you. Misty is my 120-pound, petite female Great Dane. She is grey, with black spots, and she has a great sense of humor – I'm serious. And you, reading this book, you are here in a way also. So, what do you want for Christmas? Well, you think about it for a while and I will move into my cabin.

Staying Stoned

Monday, December 25, 1978
around noon

Hello again, did you think about what you want for Christmas? I'll tell you what I want. I want to make it through this day without giving up and going home. What a drag it is being alone on Christmas, especially when you don't have any weed. Smoking grass has always been entertaining for me, even when I haven't had anything in particular to do. This morning I had plenty to do. Between plowing the road to my cabin, shoveling off the front porch, building a fire, and unloading my truck, I have been very busy. Now I am sitting here in front of the wood stove all alone and feeling sorry for myself.

Sure, there are plenty of people worse off than I am! And sure, I'm probably not the only one alone on Christmas Day. However, knowing that doesn't make me feel any better. Thoughts of people partying, opening presents, eating, and taking drugs are making me wonder what I am doing here at all. If I left now, I could be home by dark, though I know it would be the wrong thing for me to do. Most of my life I have been a non-finisher. Sometimes even a non-starter.

I was accepted at a college twice, and twice I never started. It took five years for me to complete high school, I left in my junior year and had to repeat it. In 1976, I started a small crafts store with a friend and nine months later I gave that up, leaving my friend to go it alone. Aside from my electric ice-cream scoop idea, I have built a number of products with the intention of selling them. Somehow, I never quite followed through. That is why it is so important for me to stick it out here until April.

It wouldn't be fair to blame all of my life's failures on drugs. A lot of those failures stem from the kind of person I am, lazy. Drugs and getting high do make it easier not to care about being lazy though. Like doing this book – if I were stoned right now, I would shut off the tape recorder and just think about writing a book. Before you know it, the book would be published, I would be making lots of money, appearing on the Johnny Carson's show, and negotiating with 20th Century for the movie rights. Then, I would fall asleep a star, and tomorrow I would wake up right where I was yesterday, nowhere.

Maybe this all sounds a little heavy to you? But, I need to tell myself there is a good reason for me not to get high, because I do love taking drugs. I love planning to take drugs, preparing what is needed to take them, and I love taking them and waiting for the reaction to hit me. I like pot, and acid, and mescaline, and cocaine, although I don't like the price of coke, even if it is the real thing.

Despite my desire to stop using drugs, at least for the next three months, I don't think I will ever stop liking the immediate effect that drugs have on me. Let's face it – if drugs made you feel shitty, not too many people would be using them. And, they wouldn't call it getting high, they would call it getting shitty. Wait a minute, I remember my friends and I calling getting really drunk, "Getting Shitty?" Or, "Shit faced." What an appealing concept – not!

The problem is that with some people like me, it becomes more desirable to do drugs than anything else. Often, I have found myself getting stoned, and then, trying to think of something to do that I had never done while stoned before. It's like there becomes two sets of milestones in your life. There is the first time you did something, and then there is the first time you did it stoned – the first time I went to the movies and the first time I went to the movies while stoned – the first time I drove a car and the first time I drove a car stoned – fifteen miles per hour in the passing lane and thinking I better slow down the whole time – the first time I experienced sex and the first time I made it while stoned.

So, this is Christmas? "Misty Stop! Stop that Misty!" I think my dog needs to go wee-wee. We'll be right back.

Richard Ebner

Misty was greatly relieved that I paid attention to her needs, and so am I. Christmas? I remember working on Christmas Day once. It was a Rexall Drug Store. Interesting work environment for me, don't you think?

I was sixteen-years-old at the time, and my favorite things to sell were condoms and tampons. Once a man came in and bought a box of sanitary napkins. This guy was so uptight he felt that he had to tell me they weren't for him. Another time a woman came in to buy rubbers for her husband. She insisted on talking to the pharmacist. That was her big mistake. The pharmacist asked what size her husband was and she didn't know she was being teased.

But, back to Christmas Day – I was feeling rather sickly that day. So, the pharmacist gave me some prescription drugs. Later in the day, someone else at the store took my temperature and we discovered that I had a 102* fever. After that they let me go

Staying Stoned

home. I think I had hallucinations that night. Must have been from the fever. I don't think the pharmacist was giving me hits of acid?

Did you ever drop acid? LSD, boy, that's one drug that scared the hell out of me when I first heard about it. Back in the days of Timothy Leary, the peace movement and hippies. Yeah, you know, the good old days. Well maybe they weren't the good old days for you. I'm not sure they were for me either. Anyway, back then, lots of people were tripping to become more enlightened. As opposed to today, when people trip just to have a good time. I don't know how many people actually got any enlightenment out of dropping acid. Although, that was the "in" reason to do it back then.

Being a conscientious objector to the Vietnam War, I felt I couldn't be very conscientious unless I tried tripping at least once. Trouble was, I was scared to take LSD. Having heard Tim Leary speak in favor of taking acid didn't reassure me. The guy seemed like a burn out and I wondered if LSD had done that to him.

Years went by from when I first thought of dropping acid and when I actually took my first trip. Most of the stories in the newspapers, at the time, told of people dropping acid and then thinking they could fly. They would jump out of sixth floor windows. Tales of people running all over town with two broken legs and not even knowing they were broken were real popular for a while. I wondered what demons might be lurking inside my head just waiting for LSD to put them in control of me.

Of course, even if you didn't have a bad trip psychologically, there was always the possibility of getting some bad acid – a risk you take with all street drugs. Not until a friend of mine, whom I will refer to as Guru (for his protection), spent many hours talking to me about what his trips were like, did I seriously consider dropping acid myself.

Guru said I had too stable a personality to have a bad trip and he offered to test any acid I wanted to take. By taking acid from the same batch a few days in advance of my taking it, Guru would act as a guinea pig for me. If he was still alive after twenty-four-hours or so, I figured it would be safe enough for me to try.

Time for me to make myself some lunch. Oh, I thought up something brand new, pothead jokes. They are modeled after elephant and baby jokes. Here is my first one – how many potheads does it take to make a phone call? Give up? I'll give you the answer after lunch. Also, after lunch, we will go on my first LSD trip.

Staying Stoned

Dial it up

I know you are dying to find out how many potheads it takes to make a phone call. So, here's the answer, eight. Why eight you say? Well it takes one to dial the phone and seven to remember the number. Not necessarily funny, but often true. Most heavy dopers I have known have lousy short-term memories. Something that will probably happen to us permanently when we get old, or so I'm told.

One day, not that long ago, I had some trouble remembering to bring my hammer to work with me. Not too good for a carpenter. Kind of like a cop forgetting his gun. This particular morning, I drove the six miles from my shop to where I was to be working that day. Upon unloading my tools, I realized that the masonry hammer that I needed was not with me. I then had to drive the six miles back to my shop to get the hammer I had forgotten – a reasonable mistake. Could happen to anyone, right, but three times in the same morning? Yes, twice I drove the six miles back to my shop, and twice upon arriving I could not remember what I had returned for. I picked up some other tools, and thinking they must have been what I needed, I again left for the job site – again without that masonry hammer. After my third trip back, I didn't bother returning to work that day.

Richard Ebner

Coffee, Tea, or LSD?

My first acid trip started in 1974, at eight o'clock and it ended about twelve hours later. I lived in my own apartment at the time and my friend Guru was staying with me temporarily. Guru had already tested the acid that I was to take a few days before. He tested acid from the same purchase at least. Everything was planned in advance. We had enough beer to quench our thirsts, for Guru said we would get very thirsty once we got off. There was plenty of pot around to mellow out our trips, thanks again to Guru. We even stocked in some vitamin C for the purpose of bringing us down, if we should want to come down early. I had never heard of this before, but Guru swore it worked. After all, what did I know, I had never even done acid before – and Guru was, well, my guru.

The evening started out as planned, and then, quickly, everything fell apart. Guru took from his bag of tricks our trip tickets, the LSD. That was when I had my first look at blotter. For those of you that are unfamiliar with this type of LSD, blotter is tissue paper with a spot of LSD doted on it. This particular blotter was two-ply blotter, which allowed a person to split a hit in half. It was suggested by Guru that I start by doing only half a hit, a suggestion I followed. Guru did two whole hits, telling me that because he had done so much acid in the past, he had developed a tolerance to the drug and now needed more in order to get off – something that I imagine heroin users can relate to.

After dropping the acid, which we did by allowing the tissue paper to dissolve on our tongues, we settled in to wait for the drug to hit us. Before we had gotten off, the doorbell rang. It was my brother at the door. He had just bought a new motorcycle and he wanted to take me for a ride. Now, I am the kind of person who loves to drive a good bike, but hates to be a passenger on one. Being on the back of a motorcycle scares the shit out of me. As long as I am in control, I have no fear. It is ironic, or at least out of character, that I should enjoy doing drugs. I won't get on a roller-coaster, because they won't let me drive. The merry-go-round is about the wildest ride that I can handle, at the carnival. Going fast doesn't bother me, as long as I am the one controlling the gas pedal. That need to be in control seems to be inconsistent with my use of drugs. I am almost always willing to do a drug and let it take me wherever it will – another thing for me to think about.

Back to the night in question – I didn't want my brother to know that I had just dropped acid and would be getting off soon. It seemed the easiest thing to do was to go for a ride on my brother's bike and hope he would bring me home before the

Richard Ebner

LSD started to work, he didn't – but it did.

As the LSD started to take effect, I began to feel slightly disorientated. Even though we never went more than a few miles from my apartment, I found myself wondering where I was and then realizing, I was somewhere quite familiar. I began feeling uneasy. Buildings started to take on a dream-like appearance, almost as if I were looking at them through a fish eye lens.

The streets started moving, undulating like the streets were all towels and some giants were at the ends of the streets shaking them, only in slow motion. Everything was in slow motion. Tail lights on cars left trails behind them and the head lights looked like crystals, sparkling and very bright. I figured I must have gotten off.

I remember looking down between the wheels of the bike, at a point where the rear tire met the pavement, and wondering what it would feel like to be run over. I imagined myself being run over the long way, with the rear wheel of the bike rolling up between my legs and finally over my neck and head. As the tire rolled over me, my body seemed to act like clay. It squished down flat in the middle and folded over the edges of the tire, like pie dough over a rolling pin.

There I was, folded quite in half, going around and around with each eyeball on the opposite sides of the tire starring at the other eyeball. Nothing seemed the least bit painful about the whole ordeal. In fact, there wasn't even any blood in my little fantasy. Later on, I wondered if that is how those people reported about in the news during the sixties, let themselves jump out of windows thinking they could fly. Maybe they began to believe a certain fantasy they were having and they lost the ability to separate the effects of the LSD from reality. That kind of loss of control is something I have never experienced so far.

Even though I was imagining being run over, and in my fantasy, it seemed like a fun thing to do, I didn't lose touch with the reality, that if I was really run over it would most likely kill me, and at the very least, hurt a lot. I knew that if I let myself fall in front of that tire I wouldn't just ride around the rim with a smile on my face like the Pillsbury Dough Boy.

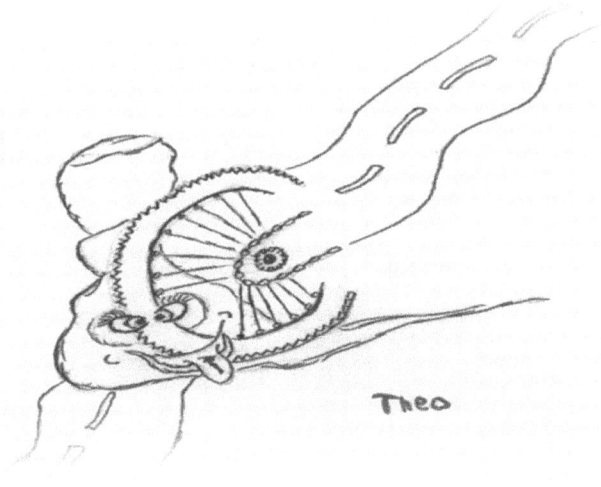

So, what made me able to distinguish between reality and fantasy, while tripping, when some others could not? I am certainly not saying that I am the only one who can – but why was I okay during that ride on my brother's motorcycle, that night? Why didn't I jump off under the tire if it seemed like so much fun? I don't know. Perhaps it is a tribute to my stable personality, as Guru put it. Although, I don't feel that my personality is all that stable.

Maybe half a hit of blotter just wasn't enough for me to go completely off the wall. Maybe I was lied to and no one ever went crazy from taking acid and jumped out sixth floor windows thinking they could fly. It wouldn't be the first time we were lied to about the effect drugs would have on us. More likely though, LSD, like everything else in life, effects different people differently. Whatever the reason, I am glad I survived intact.

By the time my brother had me back to my apartment, I was tripping quite well and feeling rather sick to my stomach also. Fortunately, my brother didn't hang around long after our ride and he left without coming in. This was good, because it meant I could let down my guard and stop pretending I was straight. I needed to tell Guru all about what was happening to me.

Once I was in my living room again, I started to feel even worse. I laid down on the couch – a mistake! Laying down caused everything in the room to spin. Much like in the past, when I had come home really drunk. Once I would lie down, I could not imagine how I could have been standing only seconds before. Only now, things in the room were not only spinning, they were distorted as well.

My apartment was in a single family Victorian house that had been converted into four units. The walls were ten feet high, floor to ceiling. And those walls were covered with fifty of my own water-color paintings. Many of these paintings were done using florescent paints. You know, the kind that glow under ultra-violet light. I also had a good supply of black-lights left over from the late sixties and early seventies. In fact, one of the light fixtures still had an "Impeachment with Honor" bumper sticker on it. If that doesn't mean anything to you, then it's a case of 'you-had-to-be-there.' Anyway, the glowing effect of the black-light paintings, coupled with the LSD in my system, caused the paintings to look as if they were moving in and out of the walls. My sense of depth perception was definitely taking a beating.

Guru had been on the phone ever since I returned from my motorcycle ride. When he got off the phone from talking to his girlfriend, he noticed I was lying down and asked if I was alright. Guru suggested I sit up. He said I needed to get my mind off feeling sick. If I wasn't having a bad trip, it certainly was becoming an unpleasant one. I sat up and talked to Guru about my little ride with my brother. He told me that his girlfriend was coming over to do some acid with us. This was to be her first trip also.

Sitting up made me feel much better and soon I felt cocky enough to take the other half of my blotter. Guru and I continued talking as we waited for his girlfriend to arrive. The conversation felt very satisfying and we seemed to understand each other better than ever before. I can't remember one specific thing we talked about, except how well we felt we were communicating. The end of every sentence by one of us was followed by the other saying – I know exactly what you mean.

After about an hour of this perfect understanding, during which we also drank several beers and smoked at least a couple joints, the doorbell rang. Guru got up to answer it figuring it was his girlfriend. It wasn't, it was mine, arriving unexpectedly. As with my brother, I didn't want my girlfriend to know I was tripping. Unlike my brother however, she was not so easily fooled. We went into the bedroom leaving Guru in the living room, in front of the television, a place where Guru often spent a good deal of his time.

The one bathroom in the place could only be accessed by going through the one bedroom. It was a layout that did not provide much privacy when sharing the space with someone else, a problem that would cause me to ask Guru to move out a few months later.

Once in the bedroom, I found out that my girlfriend wanted to have a talk about something that happened to her that day. I sat down on the bed next to her and tried to listen and act straight. The second half-hit of acid was getting to me by then.

I was feeling rushes all through my body and especially in the area of my crotch. It became more and more difficult for me to concentrate on what my friend was saying. She kept asking me why I was acting so strangely and I kept telling her that I didn't know what she meant. I let her assume that I was just very stoned. This was something she could accept and expect about me, although she didn't like it very much.

The rushes kept sending waves of some of the best physical feeling of horniness, without any outside stimulation, that I could have ever imagined. Unfortunately, for my girlfriend, I wanted to take them one step further and add some outside stimulation. At some point, I leaned over, kissed her, and began to generally feel about her body. This was very poor timing. My girlfriend got up and left, leaving me alone to grope about the pillow. The pillow threw me out of bed as well. Just not my night I guess.

I got up to take a piss. I remember saying aloud to no one in particular, for there was no one in the room with me except the pillow – "I've got to take a piss." Then I began to wonder why people say – 'take a piss', since you don't take any urine with you from the bathroom, unless you are careless. I thought, why don't we say – I am going to give a piss?

As I started giving a piss, the vibration of the warm urine passing through my penis felt very good and my cock responded by becoming quite erect. This forced an adjustment in the angle of the dangle, as they say. After making necessary adjustments, I began to stare at the stream of yellow fluid coming from the end of my penis. That is when I noticed the golden arches. The urine looked as if it was frozen in midair, like water from a hose only with a strobe light illuminating it – a golden arch. Funny and strange the things one remembers. Still today, I sometimes think of McDonalds when I am giving a piss.

Back in the living room, Guru's girlfriend had arrived, dropped some acid, and was off to a bad trip. She was very frightened. Guru was trying to calm her down. They went out on the porch to talk. I guess she felt self-conscious, with me around. Everyone kept trying to get away from me. I sat and watched TV for a while. Then it became too intense for me. All I could comprehend were the colors. And, they didn't seem to want to stay inside the set. Bright streams of blues, reds, and purples came shooting out at me.

Staying Stoned

The story meant nothing to me, if there was one. I might have been watching the news, I don't know. When I shut the TV off, the colors were still there for a long time. Or maybe they only lasted a few seconds. Time was not proceeding at any known or consistent rate. That is why I can't tell you how long it was before Guru and his girlfriend returned from the porch. When they did return, we all talked for a while. Again, I am at a loss to remember anything in particular that we talked about. I just remember that it felt good to talk to people that were also tripping and who knew that I was.

Later, I left to go to bed and to give Guru and friend some private time. Morning was just coming on, as I lay on my bed, naked and alone, listening to the birds and the traffic outside my window. I tried to masturbate, but my body was too tired. And my mind was too awake. This would become a regular problem with tripping for me – wanting to sleep but not being able too. Hours of lying in bed with the fun effects of the acid worn off, my body exhausted and my mind unable to let go and stop thinking. It is an unpleasant feeling that I am sure most everyone has felt, even those who have never tripped their brains out. By the time of this writing, I will have tripped many times. Almost every trip ended with me wanting to sleep and not being able.

Richard Ebner

Tuesday, December 26
Lonely, cold and depressed

It is beginning to sink in that I am actually doing this and that I will be alone for most of the next three months. I am worried about my dog Misty. She seems to be having even more trouble staying warm than I am. Last night I had to let her sleep in the bed with me. Did you ever try to sleep in a bed with a Great Dane? Not exactly a lap dog – although they think they are.

When I wasn't talking to you yesterday, my time was spent breaking into my cabin, burning wood, unloading my pick-up truck, and plowing the several dirt roads inside the camp grounds. Yes, I had keys to unlock my cabin – but no they didn't work. Frozen like everything else I guess in this god damn wilderness.

You know, it's really going to be up to me to stay warm this winter. I am the kind of person who loves the cold, as long as I can get inside a nice thermostatically-controlled warm house, when I feel like it – usually in about ten minutes. Three months to cut, chop, split, and freeze. I don't know if I can take it! Yes, I can. Be strong! Man, I would have made a lousy pilgrim.

It's December 26th or the 27th, I'm not quite sure. It's the middle of the night anyway and it's fucking cold. Just getting up to re-light the stoves. Shit it's cold! Can't sleep and I'm depressed.

Wednesday, December 27
11:53 AM

Well, my father called this morning, so I have the exact time, 11:53. I have come to the conclusion that part of my depression may stem from the fact that I haven't eaten anything substantial in the last two days. The only hot meal I have had was peanut butter on toast. That was on Monday. I think I'll go to the store and pick me up some supplies.

7:00 PM

Getting out of the cabin to get some food did me good. There is something very comforting about having food in the cabin, and in my stomach. Obviously, you might say? Still, sometimes things that seem obvious to the mind, don't become real until you experience them, like hunger, loneliness, and fear. I don't mean the kind of hunger when you want a hamburger and you can't find an open McDonald's. Nor do I mean that you should starve yourself to know how it feels to suffer from starvation.

There does seem to be a need though, for some kind of balance in a person's life, in my life anyway. When I try satisfying all of my needs immediately, I feel I am losing touch with some important growth experiences. My desire to do drugs is based, at least in part, on my wanting to feel satisfied or good, right away. Without drugs, it is hard work for me to feel good about myself.

When I don't eat very much for a few days in a row, in the past due to a lack of money, I feel that I learn something about myself and others. I learn to appreciate and re-evaluate my position in this world. I learn that there are a lot of starving people that I wouldn't want to trade places with, and – perhaps I learn to be a bit more sensitive. When I force myself to be alone, cut off from people that I love, I hope I will learn to love myself more.

Today at the general store in town, I felt that I loved everyone that came in sight. It felt so good just to hear, see, and talk to people. Only three days alone and already I'm a basket case you say? Well, when was the last time you spent even one day completely alone? That is twenty-four hours without seeing another human face. Not even on TV. I don't look at it as a great accomplishment, don't get me wrong. It is helping me realize, however, how alone we all are. Alone in our minds, never being able to let anyone else in – completely – even when we want to. Maybe this experience will allow me to let more of myself out and more of others in. I truly hope so.

Thursday, December 28
8:00 AM

Last night was even colder than the night before. It is just too damn cold in this cabin. So, this is it, I give up. The rest of the tapes and the pages of this book will be blank, empty, without anything on them. No, instead I think I will go to the local saw mill and buy some slab wood to burn. Slab wood is the part of the tree that gets removed before making lumber out of logs. One side is curved and covered with bark. The other side is flat. Lengths range from a couple feet to about four feet. These slabs are stacked on pallets in half cord piles. I think you can buy a half-cord for seven or eight dollars. Hope they will take a check. My cash supply is a little low after yesterday's shopping spree.

December 29
It's Friday and company is coming

My lover, my woman, and my best friend is coming to visit me for the New Year's weekend. I say – is, because lover, woman, and best friend are all one person. She called last night and surprised me with her plans. A pleasant surprise I might add, and, just did. With her will be her son and two of his friends. Should be a busy weekend.

December 30

The slab wood I bought yesterday burns great, and the cabin is nice and warm now. Seventy-two degrees in the living room. I nearly wrecked my truck though, bringing it up here. Oh yes, and they took a check. You know, New Hampshire is thought of as being quite a conservative State, and perhaps it is. However, my experience with the people here gives me a somewhat different impression. They seem to accept me as okay, unless I prove to be otherwise. The man at the sawmill just asked me if my check was good and once I told him it was, he was satisfied. No picture ID or note from my great-grandmother was necessary. True, the amount was small, but I have had banks back in Mass. refuse to accept checks for even lesser amounts.

Raisin bran and bananas for breakfast today, that's all I have to say for now. Company is coming and there is so much to do.

CHAPTER II

January, 1979

Monday, January 1, 1979
Walking through the cabin

The cabin has returned to an almost eerie silence. My company is gone now and the sounds that became familiar only last week have returned. Noises – like the propane water heater, gurgling from time to time, and the creaking of a board that is nailed across two large pine trees, as it groans when the trees sway in the wind. Solitary sounds that tell me I am alone once more. Thanks again Glenn – you forgot to sign this one.

Time to walk about the cabin now. No, not for exercise. I thought it would be nice to describe for you what the interior of my winter home is like. I think I will draw a floorplan to help you keep track of my movements. It's a carpenter thing.

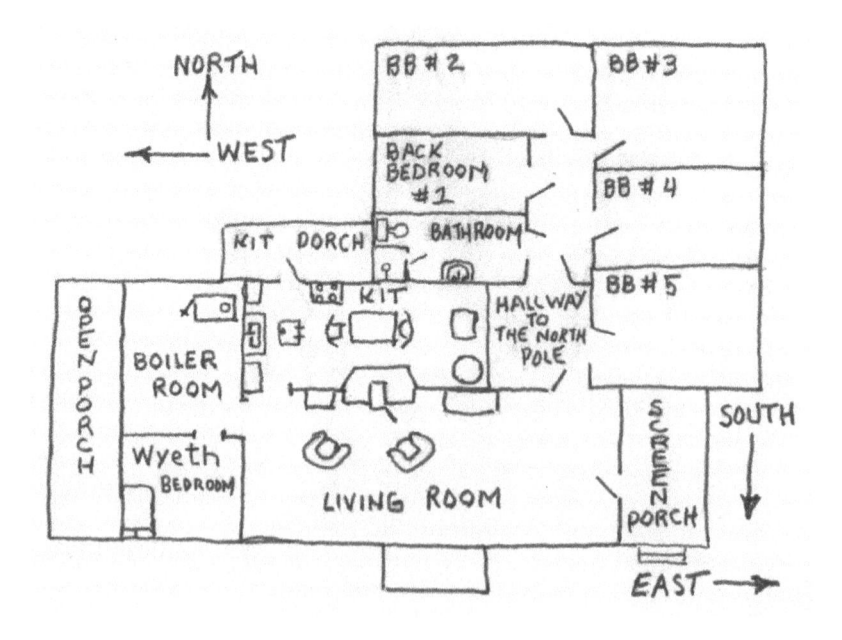

[Floorplan sketch showing: NORTH arrow, WEST arrow, SOUTH arrow, EAST arrow. Rooms labeled: BB #2, BB #3, BB #4, BB #5, BACK BEDROOM #1, BATHROOM, KIT PORCH, KIT, HALLWAY TO THE NORTH POLE, BOILER ROOM, Wyeth BEDROOM, LIVING ROOM, SCREEN PORCH, OPEN PORCH]

Look at the room marked – KIT – in the drawing, and yes, it's the kitchen. The most noticeable thing about this room is the food: twenty pounds of potatoes, twenty pounds of rice, one case of Campbell's tomato soup, three kinds of cereal, one box

Staying Stoned

of pancake mix, two loafs of bread, coffee, tea, one jar of peanut butter, a mess of canned goods, and sixty pounds of dog food. And no, I didn't draw the food.

Now that I have taken inventory, I will try to describe the less important parts of the room. Standing in the corner, wearing a white metal jacket and weighing in at twenty gallons, is the propane water heater. In the center of the room is a table with chairs – how practical. On the west wall, we find the sink and dirty dishes. Next to the sink are the cabinets for the clean dishes – those cabinets are empty. If I were to open one of the cabinets, I would have no trouble finding mice droppings. That is because the mice had no trouble finding the KIT, even without my little diagram.

On the north wall, next to the kitchen door and between the two windows is the stove. The top of the stove is covered with dirty pots and pans and more mice droppings. These country mice sure love my suburban cooking. Next to the water heater, on the east wall is the refrigerator. And you thought I was living in an uncivilized shack. Shame on you. The most interesting and unusual thing about the kitchen are the little trap doors – four small ones, with one-foot by one-foot hinged doors at the top and bottom of the north and east walls. Two of the doors open into the bathroom and two open into the hallway behind the living room. My guess is that they were made to allow heat to circulate to and from the kitchen. Sort of a crude form of centralized heating. One of the other trap doors remains to be discussed. This trap door lies on the floor, in front of the kitchen sink. It opens to a crawl space and the dirt cellar under the cabin.

Stepping out of the kitchen, to the south and turning right, we are now facing the opening to the west-wing. There are two rooms in the west wing. The bedroom is on the left, and a room that I call the boiler-room, is on the right. The boiler-room is furnished very sparsely with a couple of cots, a large wooden box for fire wood, three windows, a door that is nailed shut, and, oh yes, the boiler. Actually, it isn't a boiler but a fifty-five-gallon drum turned on its side and converted into a wood stove. This provides my sleep-heat.

Moving south once again, we find ourselves in the west-wing bedroom, or what I call the Wyeth bedroom. The Wyeth bedroom is perhaps the prettiest and coldest room, in the heated part, of the cabin. It has three windows, two of which afford a beautiful view of both mountains in the back yard. One dresser with mirror attached and a metal-framed double bed, pretty much fill up the floor space. Windows right next to the bed allow me to watch the moon and the stars at night.

Heading east a few steps puts us in the largest room, the living room. It is a dark room even during the day, with trees grown up around its southerly faced windows. In the center of the north wall is a large stone fireplace. Setting on the hearth of the fire place is my only other main source of heat, a small airtight wood stove attached to the chimney. On either side of the stove are comfy chairs. As I reminisce about my past drug use, I am talking to you while sitting in one of those chairs.

Five doors provide openings from every side of this longer than wide room. A small room behind the chairs you see, served as an entry hall before the front steps fell off. The door to that mudroom area is now nailed shut.

Richard Ebner

This cabin, and the whole camp for that matter, reminds me of a sinking ship that has its water-tight compartments closed off, one after the other, in order to prolong the inevitable. As porches, and the steps leading to them, get rotten and worn out, they are removed rather than fixed. Many buildings have collapsed all together, with only their foundations remaining. The cabin I am living in has three porches, two of which have no steps.

Back inside now – at the east end of the living room there is another door leading to a screened in porch. I use this porch to store my firewood. To the left of that door, on the north wall next to the fireplace, is a table with my stereo receiver and turntable on it. Got to have music no matter what, don't you think?

Next to the stereo is another door. This door leads to the North Pole, or so it seems. Truthfully, it opens to a hallway and the five back bedrooms. I wouldn't even open this door, if it wasn't the only way to get to the bathroom. You see, there is no heat at all in this part of the cabin. This makes for some rather chilly sprints to and from the bathroom, which is about ten feet down the hall. Slightly warmer than an outhouse, the bathroom is located next to the kitchen on the inside corner of the L-shaped jog in the cabin. It's not really a bathroom, for there is no bath. Just as well though, for the water in the tub would only freeze before I finished bathing. There is a metal lined shower stall. Don't lean on the walls while showering.

Tuesday, January 2
7:30 PM
The beaver sleeps at my house

I made the mistake today of going outside without my tape recorder and I am really regretting it now. This means I will have to tell you what happened today in retrospect. I'll try not to make this mistake in the future. Although sometimes it won't be possible to keep you with me in real-time. I only have two hands, and when felling trees, I need to keep both of them on the chainsaw.

This morning I walked over to the main house to steal,

temporarily, some cooking utensils I was missing in my kitchen. On the way back, I noticed a small animal swimming in a puddle in the road. As I got closer, it looked as if it might be a large rat. He seemed to be totally unaware of my presence as I kept moving in closer to get a better look at him.

Pretty soon Misty noticed what was going on and decided this would be a wonderful animal to chase. Small, defenseless, and slow. What more could a suburban dog ask for? Misty chased the little creature to the pine trees, with the board nailed across them. There, the rat, or whatever, made its stand. On land, the animal moved awkwardly and was no match for a Great Dane in an open-field run.

The back feet were webbed and its' front feet looked like those of a squirrel. The tail was wider than any rats tail I had ever seen, but still not as wide as the tail of a beaver. I thought – this must be an awfully small beaver, must be a baby. The animal looked like it couldn't have weighed more than four of five pounds.

Well, Misty kept barking at it and trying to get it to run again. The tiny fur-soaked beaver backed itself up between the pine trees with the board nailed across them, and every now and then charged at my dog.

I decided that, if this little creature was indeed a baby beaver, it must have gotten separated from its mother. Leaving Misty to keep it entertained, I went to get a trash barrel to capture it in. I figured that if I laid a trash barrel on its side, in front of the baby beaver, and ran around the other side of the trees, maybe I could force it into the barrel. Then tip the barrel up to trap it. With Misty's help, the plan worked perfectly!

I carried the beaver in a barrel to the screened-in porch. There, I made some closer observation and decided I needed to do some research on beavers. Going into the cabin I got the B book from my set of 1957 World Book Encyclopedias. Nothing like being up to date, not that it matters in this case. I don't think beavers could have evolved much since 1957.

As I read the description of a beaver, everything seemed to

fit, except for the size. This I attributed to it being only a baby. As described, my beaver had small eyes, thick fur, tiny ears, even the two buck teeth in front of its snout. The tail didn't look quite like the picture in the book. It was skinnier, but it was still the right shape and I figured it just hadn't grown out yet.

Reading on, I found out that this beaver was in the perfect environment for finding what it needs to eat. Birch and poplar being their favorite trees to make a meal of. This was not really a surprise to me, for I knew that beavers lived within the camp grounds. There is even a sign pointing to the beaver pond. But, this was my first up-close look at a real live baby beaver.

As I had plenty of poplar kicking around on the porch, for fire wood, I decided to cut a small piece and see if my little friend was hungry. Carefully, I stuck the poplar into the trash can. Just then, a very scared beaver was followed by an even more startled me. The innocent looking little animal jumped half way up the side of the trash barrel and bit off a piece of the small stick I was trying to feed him. He seemed more interested in my fingers than the poplar. That is when I realized I needed a more secure place to keep my new-found house guest.

I remembered seeing several different kinds of cages in the camp over the years. So, I set off on a journey to find one. My search ended at the mess hall, where I found just what I was hoping to find – a nice wire cage, with a removable top. After carting the cage back to the porch, I set off in my truck to find some mud and sticks, to make the cage homey. The mud I was able to shovel from the road at the bottom of where that road leads to what was always called the Hill House, because it was on top of a hill, and the sticks I found on a pile out behind the corral.

Once I had completed the transfer of beaver-in-a-barrel, to beaver-under-cage, I went to my cook book to see what kind of beaver recipes it provided. There weren't any. So then, I figured I would be a humanitarian instead. By calling a neighbor about a mile up the road, I was able to get the local game warden's phone number. Upon talking to the game warden, and after answering his questions about the size of the beaver, it was decided that I keep the animal overnight, until the warden could send someone out to look at it. So, for tonight, the beaver sleeps at my house.

Tuesday, January 2
7:30 PM
Things are not always what they seem

Things are not always what they seem to be sometimes. At about noon today, a shiny new car with officially looking New Hampshire State Government license plates pulled into the camp grounds. Out of the car came two large men wearing guns. They were fish and game officers, come to look at my baby beaver. After greeting them at their car, we walked around to the porch. Before I even had a chance to show them the cage, one of the men said, "It smells like a muskrat." He was right– how embarrassing!

I was told the best thing to do was to let him out of the cage, near some water. One of the officers told me that muskrats are very good swimmers. The reason their tails don't look like most rats' tails is because they are designed to be used as a rudder when swimming. I thanked the two men for coming out to see me and I apologized for my beaver being a muskrat. They told me not to worry about it – "That's our job." Once they had left I took the cage down to the brook and let the little full-grown muskrat out. He had no trouble finding the water and swimming away from this nut that kept calling him, "little beaver."

10:35 PM

Oh dear, oh deer, where oh where can they be?

I am going for walk, and that's right, you're going with me – you little black box you. Stepping outside in the cold night air brings a certain thought to mind. Those of you that have smoked grass before should be able to relate to what I am thinking about

Staying Stoned

right now. Did you ever smoke some pot and then go outside, in the fresh air, and notice that it smelled like burning leaves? I wonder why that is? The first few times it happened to me, I even looked around to see who was burning leaves, in the winter time. Strange, it doesn't smell like burning leaves tonight.

The sky tonight is the brightest it has been since I got here. The stars are so bright and so plentiful, it is almost hypnotic staring up at them. You really have to come way out in the country, like this, to appreciate how many stars there are in the sky. A city sky, or even a suburban sky, just can't make it. Too much ground light I suppose.

I can't stand here staring at the stars for too long. Misty gets cold if she doesn't keep moving. Right now, it is five degrees above zero. The radio said it will go down to about fifteen below tonight. Walking by my living room window, and looking inside, it looks so warm and cozy in there. The snow outside is that squeaky, crunchy kind. Stepping on it sounds the way hair does when you run your fingers through it, after having just washed it.

I am walking out to the gate and up the road that leads into the camp now. Going to try and find a few deer to look at tonight. There is a spot near my neighbor's house where the deer come to feed on apple mash that he puts out for them. Apple mash is a combination of apple cores and skins left over from cooking apples, when making home-made apple cider – the deer love it.

Coming to the mail box now, at this point the road into the camp meets Limekiln Road. There is a triangle here allowing you to turn left or right. I am going left, for about a mile, to where I hope the deer are waiting for me. When I started outside there was a tiny slit of a moon. Now I can't seem to find it in the sky.

I am about four hundred feet from the triangle now and I just noticed a small stream, that somehow, I had missed in all these years of coming up here. I keep hearing these snapping noises in the woods around me, like the sounds of something stepping on twigs. When I shine my flashlight into the woods the noises stop. Sometimes I think I have seen the reflection of my light in an animal's eyes. It has turned out to be just the reflections from ice particles on tree branches. Next, I'll be seeing UFOs. Kind of spooky out here. I don't know what's making the noises.

As I continue walking, uphill now, there are huge pine trees on either side of the road. They shoot way up into the sky dissolving into silhouettes against the starry night. God, it is beautiful out here!

"Misty come here! Good girl, stay with me." I have reached the spot now where there should be deer. I will have to hold Misty so she doesn't scare them off. Don't see any deer right now. I will wait here as long as I can. If they arrive, you will be the next one to know about it. Standing under a "no hunting" sign. Seems like a good place to wait.

Tea time

The deer never showed up. Or, if they did they never showed themselves to me. It got so cold standing there under the "no hunting" sign, that my fingers started to stick to the controls on my tape recorder. I am back in the cabin now thawing out. Time for a cup of tea. Don't give up on the deer. We will see them another night. This I promise.

Friday, January 5
Afternoon
Smoking on the job

The temperature went down to fifteen below zero last night, or about minus twenty-five degrees centigrade. Does this whole change to the metric system bother you as much as it does me? Converting inches to centimeters, miles to kilometers, pounds to kilograms and quarts to liters. Sometimes I wish I could just go to bed one night and in the morning when I got up everything would be metric. It might be difficult for a few months or so, but far less confusing than all this converting, I think. Instead of trying to relate metric measures to those we are familiar with, we would all just start thinking metric.

This is how things might be someday – "Would you please pick up 3.78 liters of milk and .946 liters of orange juice to go with our breakfast tomorrow?" Having been a carpenter for the past three and a half years, I am hoping to get out of the business before I have to order a 3.81 x 8.89 – instead of a 2 x 4. When you think of it though, it would be far worse if we were changing from metric to standard. Our old standard system doesn't make too much sense, even when you know it.

It has occurred to me that you may be wondering how I was able to shovel mud from the road the other day, with the temperatures being so low. New Year's Day we had a heat wave that lasted until late Tuesday night. It reached fifty degrees Fahrenheit on Tuesday and that may be what drove my beaver, excuse me, muskrat out of the water. Since then it hasn't been any warmer than the low twenties.

On almost every job I have ever worked, and I have done a lot of different things, some of the workers have smoked grass on the job. That, more often than not, included me. Sometimes I wonder what effect that has on the productivity of this country. Did Japan get that much smarter or did we just burn ourselves out with the weed? No point wondering about it too much – I suppose someone will come out with a study on it eventually.

I answered an ad for school bus driver job, just about the time I gave up my crafts store. Since I had driven many kinds of trucks, I guessed that driving a school bus couldn't be much different. Just like a long yellow truck with windows, I thought. The ad didn't give any phone number, just an address, so I jumped on my motorcycle and headed down there.

Upon arriving, I saw a dirt parking lot with about fifteen buses parked in it and a number of buses pulling out. Setting my bike out of the way, I took my helmet off and looked for an office. There wasn't one. Just a single gas pump near the garage door of a building at one end of the lot. Walking through the lot, there was a man carrying a clip board and handing out keys to drivers. He looked as close to being a boss as anything else around the place so I walked over to talk with him.

Not wanting to interrupt, I followed along behind him for a while, as he gave the drivers their keys and some brief instructions about their routes. Between this activity he mumbled and cussed over his clip board like he had some great problem to solve. When the time seemed right, I ventured to say, "I saw your ad in the newspaper and I…"

"A new driver," he said, cutting me off. "Great, here is the key to bus number six. Do you know Plain Street?" Yes, was my answer. Then I told him I didn't have a school-bus driver's license yet.

"Oh shit," he said, and then he was interrupted by another driver asking for her key. After handing out the key and looking over his clip board, for another few moments, he asked if I knew how to drive a school bus. I started to tell him how I had driven all sorts of trucks. Then he told me to take number six to the corner of Plain Street and Chelmsford Street. "There is a bus broken down there. Give the driver your bus keys and wait there until I send someone for you. And, oh, by the way, what is your name?"

"Theo," I told him. Then I asked about not having a driver's license for buses. He told me not to worry, there'd be no kids on the bus and to just be careful. Thus, started my work relationship with the Bus Company. Things were to get much stranger and even more illegal.

The next day, I was sent with one of the other drivers on a regular bus run, as part of my training. He was a large bearded man in his early to mid-thirties, with what I felt was an overly friendly hello. I sat in the front seat next to his, as he started the bus, with his foot to the floor! Soon we were leaving the bus yard with his foot still flooring the gas pedal. I hung onto the pole in front of my seat for what was to be a wild ride.

The driver was the kind of person who opened a conversation with total confidence that the person he was talking to was as interested in hearing what he was saying, as much as he was into telling it, and not caring if that proved not to be true. He began by asking me what I did before coming to work for the bus company. Then, barely pausing to hear my reply, he proceeded to tell me why he was wasting his time driving buses. Apparently, this large personage had been a cement truck driver. But, because of a slowdown in the construction industry he was laid off and collecting unemployment. Since the bus company was quite willing to pay him under the table, it was to his benefit to drive a school bus in the afternoons. I clung to the pole as he wheeled the bus around corners and down little side streets. He boasted about what good money there was in driving those big cement trucks.

About midway in our trip to school, my talkative bus driver took from his pack of cigarettes, what I thought was going to be another cigarette, for he had already smoked three during our short ride, but instead, this time it was a joint He handed it to me with a lighter.

I hesitated to light it, asking, "Do you think we should smoke this in the bus?"

Turning his head and looking at me with a stare that could set concrete instantly, he said, "You better not be one of those fucking straights!"

I thought about telling him about all the drugs I had done,

and how under most circumstances I loved to get stoned. I thought of saying that I was just worried that the kids would smell it when they got on the bus soon. I thought of these things. I said nothing. Somehow, I got the feeling he didn't want to discuss it.

I lit the joint and took a long deep drag, as if to prove I knew what to do with the stuff. After passing it back and forth a number of times, I was buzzed. It was good shit. Soon the bus reeked with the smell of pot and I wondered how my grass-smoking chauffeur was going to conceal our activities from the students soon to be entering the bus. It never occurred to me that he had no intention of hiding it at all.

Before very long, we arrived at the school. My driver, trainer, backed the bus into its space and we didn't have to wait long for the first kids to enter. Some of the kids had left before the dismissal bell to make sure they got the best seats on the bus. Usually the back or front seats were the most desirable. Soon three boys piled on the bus and greeted the driver with a slap-style handshake and a – "What's happening man?" Before they had reached the back seats, the driver called one of the boys back. Reaching into his pocket he pulled out what must have been twenty joints bound together by a rubber band. Then he asked the kid if he needed any grass. The boy said he did and gave the driver a buck for two joints. This scene was repeated several times, with other kids on the bus.

After all the sales had been completed and the buses in front of us started to pull out, we headed for the road again. Once out on the road, the driver pulled another joint from his cigarette pack and handed it to one of the kids to light. Driver and passengers smoked all the way home.

As I road along, still stoned from the ride there, I was in shock. Although I thought of myself as fairly hip to what was happening at the time, I had never heard of school bus drivers selling joints to the kids on the bus and then smoking with them on the ride. Could it really be that smoking grass had become so casual?

It is important to mention that the story I have described here was not the norm, as I perceived it. I wouldn't want you to get the impression that all school buses are smoking dens, with drivers smoking and selling grass to their passengers. Most drivers in this company, and in a subsequent company I worked for later, didn't partake in this kind of behavior. However, if it wasn't the norm, it also wasn't an isolated case. Other drivers did smoke and drink, while transporting kids, and at least one other driver I knew about, sold drugs to his passengers. I am certainly not an establishment kind of dude, but, the activity I just described seems wrong to me. And even though I never drove my bus stoned, I also never spoke up – too fearful of how it might lead back to me.

Saturday, January 6
Evening

Today was spent doing laundry, cleaning the cabin, and taking a shower. I needed one.

Sunday, January 7
Midday

The radio said it will snow today and the sky seems to agree. There is only one FM station I can receive up here with any

Staying Stoned

clarity. That is all for the best however, for the other stations I have struggled to listen to, with much wavering and crackling, are just not my style, even when I can make out their play list. Broadcasted from Vermont, this station has a very nice format. During the week, they play a combination of rock, folk, and a few country tunes. It is very rare to hear the same song played twice in one day, unless done by a different artist. A practice local Boston stations would do well to follow. Now and then they play a section of a comedy record, like Monty Python's or Steve Martin's. This works well to change the moods between different sets of music.

Most of the sets are four or five songs long without commercials. Usually songs of a set are well planned to go with one another. The station hires male and female disc-jockeys, with relaxed normal voices. Not the hyped-up, cram it down your throat with phony excitement kind of style I have become used to back home.

Well, that's not really true, I never got used to it. Maybe this human approach to broadcasting reflects the kind of audience there is in Vermont. If so, Vermont may be a nice place to live. In case you are in the area, the station is WNCS FM 93.7, Montpelier, VT. No, I don't own any stock in the station, yet.

Richard Ebner

Smoking on the job part II

Not since I was laid-off from the P.B. Inc. Company, during the oil crunch in 1974, have I had as much time to myself. My being laid off, just as winter was giving into spring, came as a not so unexpected pleasure. The job was getting to me, if you know what I mean. In two years at P.B. Inc., I had worked my way up from truck driver to shipping and receiving foreman, second shift. At one point, I had fifteen men working under me.

The problem was that upper management and I had different ideas on how to treat working people. Management didn't want me to treat each worker as an individual, with individual needs and a life outside of the work place. More on this later. For now, let me just say I was tired of fighting for the workers' rights.

If I had not been laid-off, I would have quit soon anyway. It was certainly more convenient to be laid-off. This meant I was eligible for unemployment. I was given a two-week severance pay and because I hadn't taken my vacation yet, two more weeks of pay came my way.

Let's travel back in time now to an August night in 1972. It's about 5:30 PM and it is my first night at work for P.B. Inc. – a manufacturer of synthetic materials used in the shoe industry. The personnel manager is introducing me to the second-shift foreman, my boss. I shake hands with him and he leads me up to dock #2. This is the main receiving dock for the company and it houses the foreman's office.

Two of the men, from the first shift, are still working on the dock. One man is sweeping up the concrete floor, preparing it for the second shift's take over. The other man is pushing large bins of trash out to a trash compacter, at the open end of the dock. This second man is covered with a fine white dust that makes his hair appear to be grey. Mixed in with this dust on his uniform are an assortment of different colored, thick pasty inks. Also on the floor are several men from the second shift, standing around a punch clock, waiting for six o'clock to come, so they can punch into work.

The foreman takes me into a caged-in area and closes the Dutch style door behind us. "Sit down," he tells me, as he points to a dirty metal folding chair. As I sit, I can see that he has a file with my name on it. He sits behind a desk across from me reading my file, half aloud and half to himself. At one point, he looks up at me, "I see you have truck driving experience. That is good! We just lost our truck driver."

Now he starts to get really friendly. He offers me some coffee and I refuse politely. He pours himself a cup. To the coffee he adds, four spoons of sugar and a couple scoops of powdered cream. The thought of it still makes me cringe. After some general chit-chat, during which the first shift foreman is introduced to me, my new boss says, "Come on I want you to meet the rest of the crew, before they go to their stations." As we walk out of the caged-in area, and onto the receiving dock, the men from the first shift are standing around the time clock, waiting to punch out. Most of these men are considerably older than the ones I am introduced to and with whom I'll be working. This pleases me and I wonder how many of my fellow workers smoke dope.

After the introductions, where I am introduced as the new truck driver, two of the men disappear into an elevator that opens onto the dock near where I am standing. Another man picks up where the day shift left off and starts pushing more tubs of trash towards the compactor. Three more men leave through the stairs, where I entered half an hour ago. The foreman assigns me to a young man with a goatee. He tells him to break me in on the truck. We walk out towards the open end of the dock, passing another worker, who is replacing the propane tank on his forklift. Continuing on our way, we go out through a side door and down a short flight of stairs. Backed up against one of the loading docks is an eighteen-foot GMC closed body truck. Climbing into the passenger side, my goateed instructor tells me to drive. I start the truck, pull forward, and on his instructions, turn to the right. The next thing I know, he is pulling a joint from his shirt pocket. As he lights it, he asks, "Do you smoke?" I don't answer verbally, but rather, I just put my hand out to receive the rolled weed. Now, it might have seemed strange to me, this event – ten minutes on the job and someone is offering me a joint, if it hadn't been that way in almost every work situation I had been in since I was sixteen. People smoke on the job.

Smoking the joint as we go, I am directed to another loading dock, within the same complex of buildings. Backing into this dock proves to be tricky, as I need to back around a large smoke stack, that protrudes into the alley where I need to go. There are two buildings, one on either side of the road. I manage to park the truck without hitting anything. My fellow worker, in the cab with me, says, "We call this the Old Building." Another worker has been waiting anxiously for us to arrive. When we get out of the truck, he is there. He takes the last few hits on the joint that we have been smoking. The three of us sit around the dock, near another trash compactor, and talk for a while.

I learn that my duties as truck driver will rarely take me off company property. This discovery is somewhat disheartening. And yet, it seems far better than dumping large tubs of trash, filled with sticky, ink-covered paper, into a compactor. Little do I know, at this point, that I will have plenty of practice dumping tubs later on.

Even though it is only the early seventies, already pot has

worked its way from college campuses into the mainstream of American industry. I am told that most of the second shift smokes grass on the job. "It's the only way to make it through these twelve-hour shifts, six days a week," says the man with the goatee. I ask about the risks of getting caught. Then both of them tell me not to worry – after five o'clock all the big bosses go home and the second shift foreman looks the other way, as long as you don't smoke in his face.

Monday, January 8
8:00 AM
Muskrat Soup

My favorite and only radio station was right. It snowed about seven inches, so far. Still snowing even now, as I speak to you. I plowed most of the roads through the camp last night. Later on today, I will have to plow them again. Must keep the roads open, although I don't know exactly why. It's just a habit, I guess. If it is windy and you have a kite, you fly it. If it snows and you own a snow plow, you plow. On the practical side, I do require access to the standing deadwood I need to cut down for my firewood.

Seems like a good day to cook up a batch of soup. Nothing like a big pot of soup boiling on the stove to make a real kitchen

Staying Stoned

mess. So, let's all boogie on into the kitchen. Keep that diagram handy so you don't get lost as we travel through the vast expanses of my winter mansion.

Let's see, beaver soup? No. Muskrat soup? No. Chicken soup? Yes! By chicken soup, I don't mean the canned stuff. You know, those processed soups with the world's smallest noodles, three microscopic pieces of chicken and ten times the required amount of daily sodium. This is real home-made soup we'll be making, and yes, we. Thought you could get out of cooking by reading this book, did you?

I'll just go over to the refrigerator here and get the two chicken breasts, that I bought the other day. I like to get my breasts in pairs. You can fill that five-quart pot, over there, with a gallon of water and put it on the stove to boil. Are you done? My that was fast! You're a good helper.

Now plunk the breasts into the boiling water. Plunk is a technical cooking term. Okay, add a couple table spoons of salt, sea salt, if we have it. If not, regular road salt will do. Be sure to wash the sand off though.

We are now ready for the veggies. Choice of vegetables is optional. I like to use two medium sized onions, the tops from a package of celery, three good-sized carrots, and sometimes I add a small can of peas later. You peel the onions. I am in too good a mood to start crying now.

You done? Good, now cut them into quarters and plunk them in with the chicken tits. I am peeling the carrots and cutting them into fifths, just to make this an inter-fractional meal. Ok, plunk the carrots. Be careful when plunking not to let the hot water splash on you. Now we are ready for the celery tops. This part is a bit tricky, so you better just watch. I'll need a piece of clean string. No, not that, that's my clothesline – in the draw next to the sink. Thank you.

There, now that I have the celery lashed together, you can plunk it in the pot with the onions and carrots. Since we have things properly plunked in our four-point seven three liters of boiling water (just trying to help to learn to convert) we should think of something to do for the rest of the day. The longer we let this plunked concoction boil, the better it will taste. Stirring it, once an hour or so, won't hurt either.

A cover is essential. After everything has boiled long enough, I will remove the chicken from its bones. That will be done by placing a colander, in the sink, with a pot underneath it. Then I will pour the boiled plunk concoction through it. It is most important to remember to put a pot under the colander. Many a day's boiling has served to only feed the hungry leeching field, by forgetting that important step.

Once this is done, I will remove the bones and re-plunk the veggies. The chicken meat will be added to each individual bowl of soup. All that will remain to be done, then, is to boil some rice or noodles, as tastes prefer, and add them to the plunk concoction. Oh yes, I almost forgot! Remove the string, unless you are serving your soup to Laurel and Hardy.

Tuesday, January 9
10:30 PM

Today was a serious work day. I needed more fire wood for the stoves. The sky was clear and temperatures were in the twenties. The slab wood I bought burns well, but much too fast. That discovery sent me on a search for some standing dead wood. Ever try to tell a dead tree from a living one, in the winter time, when there aren't any leaves on them? It's not so easy.

Anyway, chainsaw in hand, I went out and cut me a mess of wood. I cut about a cord, I think. It should last me a whole week, at my present rate of consumption. At this point, I think I should explain that this is my first experience at using wood, as a sole source of heat.

Richard Ebner

Back in my teens, my parents had a house with a fireplace. It was nice to sit around the crackling fire and dream about being a pioneer. At night though, when you went to bed, there was always that thermostat connected to the gas furnace to rely on. Fireplaces in suburban homes are not much more than pleasant diversions from television. Keeping the suburban home fires burning, did not provide me with much training or understanding about wood burning for survival.

I don't want to leave the impression that I went into this wilderness totally unprepared either. I did research the wood stove market before coming up here, a big job in itself these days. For my living room heat, I chose an Upland model seventeen, airtight, cast iron woodstove. Airtight stoves allow you to control the rate of burning and cast iron holds the heat longer than sheet steel.

Since I could only afford to buy one stove, to heat the bedroom I use the fifty-gallon oil drum that had been converted into a woodstove by some other fool, who stayed here one winter. I bought – a chain saw, an axe, and gasoline for the chain saw, before moving in. I also spent a few weekends here cutting what I thought was a lot of wood. I split and stacked the wood on the porch. During the first three days here, I burned most of it – hence, my buying the slab wood. For storm windows, I stapled plastic over the window glass. So, you can see, I didn't come up here only half-baked, maybe three-quarters baked.

Back to my serious work day and the search for standing dead wood. My search was very successful. I found two oak trees and two pine trees to cut down and cut up. Wonder where the expression "cut up" comes from? Cut down seems obvious. But, why cut up? Oh well, some of this wood is in the stove now and my cabin is a nice, toasty warm, seventy-two degrees. This, despite the radio telling me that it is only five above zero outside.

Tuesday, January 9
11:15 PM
Let's go out for a walk before bed – what do you say?

So far, our little walk has taken us out to the mailbox. I checked the mailbox early this afternoon and the postman hadn't come yet. Low and behold, what's this? There is mail in my mailbox. A first. I'll just take this mail back to the porch and then I think we will head up one of the trails to the base of Sugar Loaf Mountain, if I last.

It sure is cold out tonight, very well moonlit though, should be an interesting walk. The last several nights I have heard a pack of coy dogs howling. It has sounded as though there are a dozen or more of them.

There, the mail is back on the porch. Wasn't that quick?

As I take in the sky and the moon, the mountains in front of me, the reflections of the moonlight on the snow, the shadows from the trees running across that moonlight, I can't help but think about what things were like, when I was a young child. Why is it that when you are a child, you don't need any artificial stimulus? Just the natural surroundings are enough to get you high. Natural surroundings like the one's I have here in front of me now.

Whatever happened to my excitement of greeting a new day just because it was a new day? The pleasure of really feeling what the weather is like, without worrying what tomorrow might be like. Back then, I didn't need a joint or LSD to get high, my imagination was enough. Never did I say, "The weekend is coming, better pick up a case of beer so we can party." Where did my instinctive understanding of life go? When did I lose that natural high of being a child and why couldn't I sustain it?

Now that I haven't smoked any grass for a couple of weeks or gotten drunk, or done any of those adult-like things adults do, I am starting to have a renewed appreciation for the basic pleasures in life. I only hope I won't lose them again, when I return to the 'real' world.

Misty is going crazy, as she tries to guess which road I am

Staying Stoned

going to take. She darts up the road ahead of me and when she comes to the fork, she turns to see if I am still following. We are on one of the dirt roads in the camp that runs along a group of buildings called the "Barracks." The Barracks are three buildings lined up next to each other about twelve feet apart.

Two of the Barracks are about one hundred feet long, each. The third is about one hundred and seventy feet long. These buildings were used to house the workers when this was a CC work camp. Since those days, they have been converted into housekeeping units. Three to four units per building. Each unit has a cook stove, refrigerator, a sparsely furnished living room, two bedrooms, and a bathroom. Nice places to stay in the summertime. Must be damn cold in there now though. Oops, I see one of the windows is open. I'll just step off the road here and try to close it. Well, I guess it will just have to stay open, if I push on it too hard, I am afraid I will break the glass.

We are coming up on the corral now, with Black Mountain in the background. During the summer, there are about twenty riding horses milling about. The owners never close the gate to the corral, so, if you stay here in the summer, be prepared for the gift, of looking a horse in the mouth, at any time, day or night.

Richard Ebner

You might think it fool-hardy to walk around in the woods at night alone, when there are Coydogs and quite possibly bears around. I don't want you to be too afraid for me though, I do have some protection with me. On my left hip, I have strapped a hatchet and on my right hip I have a 357 magnum – maybe not the most powerful handgun, but possibly a close second. The gun is on loan from my brother. The hatchet is mine. When he loaned me his pistol, I could tell he had reservations. He wasn't worried about accidents. After a few practice lessons at his house he saw that I was capable. His concern revolved around the potential of my intentionally harming myself. So, I reassured him by saying, "Dear Brother, suicide is something that is best to be left for the next day, and the next, and so on and so on." I have never seriously considered killing myself, although as my father often proclaimed, "Never is a long time that hasn't happened yet." Our father is an atheist and a General Semanticists – words and how you use them are of paramount importance to him.

Of course, the case could be made that excessive drinking, drugging and smoking are all forms of suicide – albeit slower forms than putting a gun to one's head. Another reason why my isolating here in the mountains is a positive step towards bettering my physical and mental health. Negativity has no home here!

I would really dread having to shoot anything living, at this point, in my life. At the same time, I wouldn't want a Coydog or a bear eating me up, or my Misty. Last week, I made some paper targets and spent some time practicing shooting at them. I am a reasonably good shot.

We've completed the circle around the back side of the corral and have come to a point in the road where we can either go left back towards the camp grounds or right to the mountain trails. Let's go right! The snow is about a foot deep on the trail, since it is not plowed – can't plow the whole woods. It is soft snow on top, with a crust underneath that keeps giving way under my feet, not too hard to walk in though.

Misty is up the trail a couple hundred feet playing Indian scout. This is quite an experience! I am standing in a spot that is like right out of a fairy tale story book, enchanted forests and all that. We had a bit of an ice-storm combined with the last snow and all the trees are heavily laden. The branches are hanging over the trail, forming an icy tunnel, and the moonlight trickles in between the branches, lighting my path with an eerie shadowy glow.

Next to the trail, on our right, the ground slopes down to a brook and eventually to the beaver pond. On the left, the ground inclines very steeply towards Black Mountain. You really should come here for a walk in the winter woods sometime!

My dog is again wondering which way I am headed. At this point in the trail, there is another fork. To the left, the trail goes to the first meadow, on Black Mountain. Following along the trail, straight ahead, takes you to the base of Sugar Loaf Mountain. Misty doesn't know it yet, but we are going to go straight.

If there are any wild animals out here right now, they are probably wondering who is this jerk walking along with his dog, and talking into a little black box. "Misty, stay with me!" I must remember to repair the snow shoes that I found in the camp store. If the snow gets any deeper, it will be hard to take these midnight walks in the woods. It's just a fairy land out here. Beautiful doesn't even begin to describe it!

There is a slight tinge of fear in me, as I start to leave all signs of civilization behind. Even though it is isolated back in the camp grounds, the buildings tend to make me feel safe. Out here things have remained pretty much the way they were before people. Nary a telephone pole in sight, just trees and snow and sky. It's more beautiful than frightening.

I know you won't be able to hear my puffing into the tape recorder – but, I am puffing. Going up a steep hill now.

Oh, civilization has returned. I forgot about this old shack up here. The building has a lot of character somehow. I don't know what there is about it, but maybe it is the way it has blended with the environment. There are no windows, just holes where they once were. No doors either. Most sections of its tin roof remain intact with only one corner missing. It has been here as long as I can ever remember. Seems to have always been in this same condition too, just about ready to fall apart. Yet, every year it is here.

Gee, I hope the recorder is still working, sometimes the cold jams it up. We have made it to a level piece of ground and the terrain is a little bit different here. There are low growing bushes on both sides of the trail. To the right of me, there is a gully about thirty feet deep and fifty feet across, with the bushes growing down into it. On my left, the bushes run for a couple hundred feet, where they are bordered by thick woods. These bushes are almost completely covered with snow, except where some of the longer branches stick up out beyond the snow. This creates a sharp contrast between the moonlit snow and the bushes' branches, which look almost black.

I don't see any tracks in the snow, except Misty's. This looks like a good spot to stop and fix my boot. My socks have slid down over my heels. The boots keep chafing me.

Neither words, nor even pictures, can tell what it is like to be here right now! Feeling it is the only way. Since words are all I've got, here it goes. There is a slight breeze blowing and even though it is about five below zero, I'm not cold. I guess I am warmed up from all the walking. Around my face, the only uncovered flesh, it feels a little numb. The moon is nearly full and sharing the sky with it are thousands and thousands of tiny stars, and just a few thin clouds. On the ground are stars of

Staying Stoned

another kind, ice crystals that reflect the moonlight. As I sway back and forth focusing on the same spot, in the snow, it is like hundreds of little lights turning on and off.

When the breeze gently blows, wispy trails of snow dust come trickling down from the trees above. Mostly though, the trees just stand there, iced in snow. Even though I know it is bitter cold out and that a person could not survive long outside in this environment, it looks so inviting, so soft. It even looks warm. Like you could just lie down anywhere and have a nice comfy bed in which to snuggle and pull the snow over you as a blanket.

Birch trees have a particular advantage for being noticed on a moonlit night like this, with their white trunks forming vertical lines on the dark woods behind them. All the leaf-bearing trees, their leaves gone now, form crisscrossing lines in the sky wherever they extend beyond the horizon. Every now and then, a star will peek out, from behind one of the branches.

It is hard to decide which trees are the most beautiful here. The evergreens certainly add their share of beauty, with their arms stretched out cradling the white snow. It is really the diversity of all these trees that makes it so lovely here. It is a shame we can't appreciate that kind of diversity in human beings. The world would be such a nice place to live in if we could.

Richard Ebner

I am not going to talk to you on the way back to the cabin. Rather I am just going to think about everything I have been seeing and feeling and try to write you a poem about it. Somehow, in poetic form, I can express my feelings more succinctly, than with all the added verbiage that talking seems to create.

Wednesday, January 10
6:15 AM
A poem to the woods

WE WALKED IN YOUR SPLENDOR LAST NIGHT, MY DOG AND I.
YOU STOOD THERE SO PROUDLY, WITH ALL YOUR RELATIVES
    AROUND.
I BREATHED THE COLD AIR THAT SURROUNDED YOU,
AND VIEWED THE ICE THAT WEIGHED HEAVY ON YOUR LIMBS.
YOU WERE SO BEAUTIFUL, SOFTLY SPEAKING WITH THE WIND, IN
    THE PEACE OF THE NIGHT.
YOU MADE MAGNIFICENT SHADOWS, ON THE MOONLIT SNOW
    AROUND YOU.
SO GREAT IS YOUR STRENGTH, TO STAND ALL NIGHT IN THE COLD,
    WITH NO COMPLAINTS.
AND, SO DEEP IS YOUR BEAUTY, IT MADE MY HEART SWELL, JUST TO
    LOOK AT YOU.
EVEN WHEN YOU DIE, YOU WILL STILL STAND FOR MANY A YEAR,
GIVING YOURSELF, AS HOME TO OTHER LIVING THINGS.
YOU ARE FOOD, YOU ARE WARMTH, YOU ARE SHELTER.
YOU WILL ALWAYS REMAIN MY WINTER WOODLAND DREAM.

Thursday, January 11th
7:00 PM

I played some of the tapes back today to see how things sounded. When I got to the section about my midnight walk in the woods, I had an unexpected shock. It would seem that because of the cold, my battery powered tape recorder was not recording at the proper speed. This meant that when I played the tapes back, using house current, my voice was speeded up, making me sound like a chipmunk talking through his nose. I am most glad that it will not affect the printed word, as it might have spoiled the mood. Even though it was a very serious moment for me, I could not help but laugh at the strange change in my voice.

Also, I had an unexpected visit today, from two male teachers and twelve of their students. They were members of a nearby school that came to climb Black Mountain. It surprised them to find me here, as much as it surprised me, to have them arrive. Good job teachers!

Friday, January 12
10:30 AM

I am sitting down to talk with you right now, more for my benefit than yours. This morning I just need to tell my troubles to someone. As I was trying to cook my breakfast this morning, the hot water heater started to behave strangely. For some reason, it wasn't getting an even flow of gas. Maybe it was the extreme cold last night – minus twenty-five degrees Fahrenheit.

Anyway, it kept sputtering and then it would flame out. While I was attending to this problem, the water pipes in the bathroom burst. Apparently, they had frozen during the night and when they thawed out, they were broken from the expanding pressure. Panic set in! I raced through the living room and down the hall to the bathroom. When I opened the door, I found water spraying from three places.

Remembering that there are no shut-off valves in the bathroom, I raced back up the hall and through the living room again, to the kitchen. This cabin has only one shut-off valve for the water supply and it is located under that trap door in the kitchen. The handle to the trap door has long since broken off. This means, you need to pry it up with a strong screwdriver.

Of course, the screwdriver I needed was out in my truck. I quickly ran out to my truck, without my keys. Why I bother to lock my truck up here is not entirely clear. By the time I finally got the water shut off, several gallons had sprayed out. And, my breakfast burned onto the frying pan.

Now, if I had been in a down mood, this might have been enough to make me leave and find a motel. As it was, I was feeling pretty good, when I got up this morning that is! You know what I will be doing today. 'Playing plumber perhaps?'

Wednesday, January 17
10:00 AM
Parents, teachers, and administrators beware

That's right, it is Wednesday and the last time I talked to you was Friday. No excuses, I just didn't feel like talking. Did you ever feel that way? Like when the teacher would call on you for an answer and you just didn't feel like saying anything. Sure, sometimes it was because you hadn't done your homework or you just weren't paying attention. Sometimes we don't talk because we are turned inward and have nothing to say. For the last five days, I have been turned inward.

Right now, I would like to talk about some of my experiences and some of my opinions of public education. During the next section, it would be easy for me to try to blame all of my problems with drugs on the public education system in Chelmsford. In fact, there are those who, after having read this, will say that is just what I have done, even though that won't have been my intention.

During most of my four and a half years at Chelmsford High School, I was bored stiff. In order to cope with this boredom, I got stoned a lot. From my first Junior year, until I graduated, I was stoned more than I was straight. Many times, I would get stoned in my car, on the way to school, or in the parking lot before classes. Often, I didn't bother to go to school at all, once having gotten stoned.

After Christmas vacation, of my first junior year, I quit school to try working for a while. I can still remember the smell of alcohol on the principal's breath the day he questioned my motives for wanting to leave school. How could I believe he knew anymore about life than I did? Later on, in my senior year, after having repeated my junior year, I had a talk with my guidance counselor that also stands out in my memory. She had just learned of my early acceptance to college, when she stopped me in hall and said, "Congratulations, I meant to call you when you dropped out during your junior year. Glad to hear you are doing better!" She – meant to call? So, why didn't she?

Even though my senior year was better than previous years, I still spent much of my time at school stoned. During one term, I spent an entire month stoned at school. I would hit the boy's room after each class, to restore my high. Any former teachers of mine might be saying: "So, that is what was wrong with him." To this I answer, that, my being stoned was only one of a number of symptoms of the problems with public education. At the root of those problems are boredom and distrust.

Boredom caused by uncreative teachers, kept in their jobs,

by an outmoded tenure system. Frustrated teachers who once may have been good, but gave up on school systems that seem to care more about football than education.

The community, parents in particular, share a large part of the blame, for the boredom in school. Why is it that ten percent of the town seems to make all the decisions? Where are all the parents, in between report cards?

And yet, we the students are to blame, as well. Imagine what it is like for a teacher to face a roomful of stoned-faced kids and still find meaning in trying to teach them. But, if students are part of the problem, they are also mostly victims of it. After all, we haven't grown up yet. You parents, teachers, and administrators are the examples of adulthood.

It wouldn't be fair to characterize all teachers, as uncaring or disinterested. Some rare individuals did try to make school a fascinating place. And, their classrooms were an oasis, in the deserts of boredom. Unfortunately, this type of teacher usually didn't last long. Either they got tired of trying to buck the system and left, or the administration found some convenient way to get rid of them. I don't think it was a conscious attempt by administrators to weed out all the dynamic and creative teachers, but rather, a fear of losing the status quo.

People who think that they have made it, like high school principals, superintendents, and school board officials, seem to be saying: "This is the way we did it and if you are good and follow the rules, you too can obtain power and status someday." Well, power and status are useless achievements unless they are used to help improve people's well-being.

One excitingly dynamic teacher I had in my senior year was promoted out of contact with his students. Almost all of us in his class, knew the day he told us of his promotion, that it was just a move on the part of the administration to get rid of someone that they couldn't accept or manage. Only the idealistic nature of this very fine teacher prevented him from seeing the true nature of his promotion.

Two years after his promotion, I learned that he quit in frustration. They had made him head of the media department, then cut his budget so that he had next to no contact with any students. True, there could be other reasons he quit. However, when teachers of this caliber leave public education, we are left with the ones who give the same tests, year after year. Easy for them to correct and easy to cheat on, but hardly a boon to education.

Boredom among the youth in the community is a tough thing to eradicate, especially when so few adults seem interested in doing anything about it. Sports activities like Little League baseball are fine. Still, not every kid is a baseball player. If adults are truly worried about their children using drugs, they must put in the time and energy necessary to provide alternatives to drugs. Apathy among adults creates distrust with youth. Adults only seem to pay attention to the problems of being young, when the youth rebel against boredom and neglect. Vandalism, drinking, and drug abuse seem to get an adult's attention, even if it is in a negative way.

So many parents only seem interested in their child's schooling at report card time. With their heads buried in their own troubles, they are shocked when they find out their child is failing or just hasn't been going to school at all. Then they start blaming. Either it is a bad influence from the kid's friends or the kid is lazy or it's marijuana. Be aware, parents, teachers, and school officials alike, it is not pot that is messing up your kids' lives. Rather, it is an insensitive society that defines success in terms of how much money is in your bank account, or how many credit cards you have in your wallet.

Pot is only one means of escaping, for a time, a life that seems to have little meaning outside of images. Images like being a bank president, a father, a mother, or an engineer. These are positions in life that don't express all of the individual's needs.

Only in the early years of schooling did I find a wide-spread attempt by teachers to make education a personal experience. This is probably because society expects children to need nurturing. All too fast, we want our children to grow up and become forgotten adults, like ourselves.

If grade school children need nurturing, high school and junior high school students need it all the more. These young adults are moving from the carefree days of childhood into the stresses of an adult world. Does anyone really care?

Being a youth of seventeen is much like being a woman before the woman's liberation movement. You are only important as an object in someone else's control. You feel powerless. As long as you conform to an adult's standards of behavior you are rewarded for being good. These rewards are usually in the form of some material item, such as the proud father who gives his son or daughter a car upon graduation. But, of what is this father proud? Proud that his son or daughter has really learned something, or proud that he or she has climbed one more rung in the success ladder?

And for this child who buys into this system of material rewards, what has life got to offer? A good job, a new car – every three years, a wife, a husband, a thirty-year mortgage and two-point-three children, two or three weeks of vacation a year, if the child is a male, and no vacations if the child is a female. Then, when the child is thirty or forty or fifty, the world falls apart. Husband and wife find they don't really satisfy each other. They don't have any real relationship with their two-point-three kids. Their jobs don't interest them and they only go to work to maintain all the material things that they have been conditioned into thinking they need. Sounds cynical you say? Then you explain the high divorce rate, suicide, and stress-related diseases that kill.

So, what happens to the child that rebels? Maybe this child turns to drugs or alcohol, at an early age, like twelve or younger. Perhaps she or he drops out of school. Maybe, this child grows up moving from job to job never really feeling secure at anything. Society looks at this child and says, what a failure. But, maybe, this child has found out early on, what the other child discovered at thirty or forty or fifty.

Don't be left with the impression that I think the idea of family is bad, quite the contrary. Family, in its various forms, is vital to the preservation of an endangered species, the human being. So, what have I been flapping my gums about then? The need for recognition of the individual and the need of tolerance for the differences in people.

Next to nuclear destruction and environmental warming, drugs are perhaps the single most threatening problem facing this country today. I know that they are still the biggest problem in my life right now, ten years after my first experience with them.

What can parents do to help? Drive your children to school

and lock them up when they get home? This is hardly practical and certainly not helpful. Try to understand that each person is an individual and that this business of growing up is a very scary thing, for most of us. If you are brave, and I don't recommend this for everyone, you might try smoking pot with your child sometime, if he or she is already using it. Not for the purpose of condoning its use, but rather, as a way of bridging the gap in your understanding. No, better not, for that is illegal, just like cheating on your taxes, only the penalties are more severe.

Talk with your children about how life also scares you sometimes. Let them know that no matter how tough things seem to get, that you are there to support them. I don't mean support in any material sense, although that is certainly important also. I am focusing on support as the nurturing of a person's uniqueness. If your child comes home and tells you that he or she is having trouble with a teacher at school, don't just assume it is your child's fault. Let your child know that you also have trouble dealing with people sometimes. Use an example, if you can, to let your child know that you too have felt what he or she is feeling and that you understand what they are going through.

It is not enough to just love your child, for unless you show it, in some perceivable way, your child may never know you care. Reach out and take an interest in the things that effect your children. If you don't, they will turn to anything that helps to relieve the pain and ease the stress of growing up. Maybe, if I had all the nurturing I needed, I wouldn't have felt the need to smoke pot, drink alcohol, and do all the other drugs I have done during the last ten years.

To you teachers out there, who still care, I really sympathize with you. Your job is extremely underrated, underappreciated and underpaid. Complicating your job are parents that don't take an interest in education, except for how the costs effect their property taxes. You must deal with parents who you only see when their child is in trouble and sometimes not even then.

There are administrators that are only concerned with the ship running smoothly. And, as if that were not enough, there are those disinterested drugged-up students. What can you do in the short amount of time that you have a student to try and offset the effects of a seeming uncaring world? I don't know for sure. I do know things that some of my teachers did, that got through to me. You need to establish trust with your students. Keep in mind, that you are viewed by many students as the enemy, keeping them from doing what they think they would rather be doing with their time than being at school, and enforcing more rules.

Until you can convince students that you really care about them, as individuals, and not just names in a plan book, they will distrust and discredit much of what you tell them. Try putting your desk in the back of the classroom, instead of up front like the lord and master.

If you teach English, don't make your students read the classics just because they are classics and you had to read them. Through class discussions, or even a mock trial you can show how Shakespeare's Hamlet is still relevant. Stress the importance of how authors capture the basic emotions of people that have remained pretty much unchanged over the years, through their characters. Don't be too concerned if your students don't remember Achilles. Be more interested that they understand that when he said, "My lord Odysseus spare me your praise of Death. Put me on earth again, and I would rather be a serf in the house of some landless man, with little enough for himself to live on, than king of all these dead men that have done with life…," he was longing for the family that he loved and was separated from. It would not take much imagination to show how those feelings relate to every one of us.

If history is your bag, don't be afraid to deviate from the text book. If it is true that history repeats itself, then there is something wrong in the way we teach it. The perceptions, of how and why things happened in the world the way they did, seem to change much faster than history books change. Open your classroom to discussions. Don't over stress the importance

Staying Stoned

of dates, only a historian really gives a shit about them anyway, and the students that want to become historians will remember them.

When teaching sciences, inspire your students with the wonders of scientific discoveries. Don't be a pompous ass presenting all you know as fact. The more we learn, the more we realize how little we know. Demonstrate to your students how the world is becoming more and more interdependent, because of the advances in technology. Show them that even science teachers laugh, make mistakes, and sometimes don't understand things.

Math teachers – can't leave you out. If when teaching algebra, try to make your word problems relate to something your students might actually have experienced, or likely will experience soon, in their lives. I loved geometry, because I am a very visual learner, but not everyone is. As a carpenter, there is nothing like a three-four-five triangle to insure you your construction project is square! Plum, level, and square have been then principals of building from the pyramids of Egypt, to the sky-scrapers in New York. Make numbers relate to kid's lives, the world around them, and you have done your job well!

And you, gym teachers, oh, you, gym teachers, don't punish the non-athletics of the world because you were not talented enough to get into professional sports. I was always fortunate enough to be able to perform reasonably well athletically. And, I have a good deal of empathy for those who cannot. Working to have, and maintain a fit, healthy body is certainly a good goal. However, being able to score goals is not all that important. Provide alternative forms of exercise, like yoga for those students that have trouble with the All-American sports.

Guidance counselors stop telling kids what they won't be able to handle. Stop trying to fit students into schedules that are convenient for your paper work. Let students explore – the future of their whole lives may depend on it. Don't pressure kids into deciding what they want to be for the rest of their lives. Did you know that you would be a guidance counselor when you were fifteen?

School principals, stop looking around to see if your ass is covered. Don't be getting your kicks by playing police chief. Get back into the classroom once in a while, so you don't lose touch with the whole purpose of education.

School boards stop looking for people to blame and teachers to burn. This should not be a job for people with political motivations looking to make a name for themselves. Instead, they should be people who will concentrate on getting enough money to hire, creative, innovative people to teach.

If parents, teachers, and administrators can do some of these things and more, maybe future generations won't need drugs to feel turned-on, as in my case. End of this rant. Thanks for listening. I usually just try to ask question, as I have many, but sometimes I get carried away and think I have the answers – I don't!

Thursday, January 18
3:00 PM

Seven more inches of snow fell last night. I was going to cut down a few more, dead trees today, but high winds have put that off. Predictions of twenty below zero, with a wind chill factor of minus sixty-five have been made for tonight. After plowing the roads in the camp this morning, I shoveled snow up against the foundation. The added insulation of this snow should help cut down on the drafts coming through the floors. Snow is blowing across the camp grounds right now, in great swirls. Even the largest tree branches are whipping about in the wind. I can't see either of the mountains now. In fact, I can barely see any of the other buildings, in the camp. Misty thinks she wants to go out, until I open the door. Then she backs up and starts barking at me, as if to say, "You make it stop, or I am never going out again."

Richard Ebner

Friday, January 19
Almost noon

Last night was quite possibly the coldest one so far. Once again, I am very nearly out of wood to burn. It is amazing to me – the huge quantify of wood needed just to heat four rooms, in this extreme cold. It makes me wonder how the early settlers ever did survive. When I think of cutting all that wood by hand and not having the advantages of a four-wheel-drive pick-up truck, and a chainsaw, I don't think that I would have been one of the survivors. Today I will have to cut down a few more trees and I suspect I will have to do some more plowing. The high winds of yesterday and last night must surely have caused drifting. Even though I need wood badly, it will have to wait for a few minutes. Today is turning out to be sunny and bright. A perfect time to go for a walk.

We are outside now, well almost outside, I am standing on the screened-in-porch, where I keep my firewood, when I have any. The porch is about eight feet wide and ten feet long. There are three wooden benches, in the porch, an old wooden lawn chair, my aluminum step-ladder, my chain-saw, a two-gallon can of gasoline, and lots of sawdust on the floor.

Stepping outside for real now. We are in, what I call, my

back yard. Standing here, evenly spaced between the two mountains, is like standing on the belly of a huge body, with breasts rising off in the distance in front of me. The two mountains are a little bit different in size and shape from each other, which is consistent with the nature of breasts, I guess. Black Mountain is a little taller and a bit more massive than Sugar Loaf. Sugar Loaf mountain has more of a pointed top than Black Mountain.

From this point, I can see all the buildings in the camp. Looking to the southeast, set up on a hill, is what has been appropriately named the Hill House. Setting up there, all by itself, the Hill House contains three housekeeping units for the people who want to get away from it all. When I was a wee little baby, my family would stay there in the summer and sometimes mice would crawl into my crib at night and visit with me. But that's another story.

I am cutting across the snow, which is deeper than I thought – must fix those snow shoes! We are heading southeast, towards Black Mountain and the Barracks. As I suspected, the wind did cause the snow to drift and I will have to plow the roads over again. Back on one of the roads now, and directly in front of us is a telephone pole with some signs nailed to it. These signs are about two inches tall and vary in width. The top one reads, "Lime Kiln," and there is an arrow pointing, in the direction of the lime kiln. The next four read in order, "Office, Pond, Camp Store, and Corral," all with arrows. On the map, near the beginning of the book, the owner's house is also called the office, and my cabin is also referred to as the Gate House – in case you are getting lost – just go back to Theo's Map – not the surveyor's map.

Now this is interesting. A few feet away from the telephone pole, there is a drift of snow that looks like a white Hershey's Kiss.

I just slid down the embankment and dropped you into a snow drift. Sorry about that! Here, let me brush you off. There that's better. We are now standing in front of the middle Barracks Building. There is a door in front of us and over the door another sign reads, "Women." No, that doesn't mean there are women in there, it is the women's public showers, during

Staying Stoned

the camping season. Lime Kiln Camp is also registered as a youth hostel. Not everyone who comes here stays in a unit with its own shower. Many young campers stay in tents and then need a place to freshen up.

Let's walk down between two of these buildings now, for I am curious to see their actual length. Earlier I think I said two of the buildings were about a hundred feet long, each. Let's see if I was right. I am going to use my size twelve boots to measure. Here it goes – one, two, three, four, …one hundred and fifteen, one hundred eighteen, nineteen, twenty. This building is one hundred and twenty, size twelve, boot steps long. Wasn't that fun? It's time to work now. I'll talk to you later.

Saturday, January 20
10:30 AM

Cloudy and mild, if twenty degrees can be called mild. Since I got a late start at cutting wood yesterday, I will be at it again today. More snow is expected tonight, with a switch to freezing rain by tomorrow. Cutting trees in lightly falling snow doesn't bother me, in fact, I rather enjoy it. Cutting trees in freezing rain is another story altogether. I can't think of anything I like to do in freezing rain, except staying inside by a nice warm fire. If I want to have something to make a fire, I had better get to work.

Richard Ebner

Sunday, January 21
4:30 PM
Just going out to get the paper, be right back

I am headed into town to get a few supplies, including a Boston Globe newspaper. I met two women today that are weekend neighbors. They built a one room cabin about a mile east of here, down Lime Kiln road, towards the town of North Haverhill, New Hampshire. For the past several years, they have been coming up on weekends, to get away from city life in Boston.

When I first met these women today, the town plow had packed snow in behind their little Fiat. They were attempting to dig it out, when I came by with my truck. I helped them get their car out and they invited me inside their cabin, for a hot drink. It is a charming little cabin, with a central fireplace, a deck on two sides, and a sliding glass door leading out to one of the decks.

We talked for a while and when they heard that my snow shoes were broken, they offered to loan me a pair of theirs. Well, wasn't that nice of them! Now I don't have to fix mine. Since I was planning to go into town later today, I asked them if there was anything they would like me to get for them. They told me that they had decided not to drive back to Boston, because of the ice storm. But since I was going into town anyway, they would love to have a Boston Globe. So, just going out to get the paper, be right back.

Sunday, January 21
8:00 PM

Well, I'm back, but what is normally a half hour trip took almost three hours and nearly cost me my pick-up truck and potentially my life. It all started about three years ago. This is when I began developing my smug attitude about winter driving. It is also when I got my first four-wheel drive vehicle. Since owning a jeep, three years ago, and now my truck, I had begun to drive around thinking there was no amount of snow or ice that could stop me – sadly I was mistaken.

After chopping ice off my truck for about fifteen minutes, I started her up and headed out to Lime Kiln road. Lime Kiln road is a dirt, I should say, ice covered road, that in the winter time is plowed just wide enough for two cars to pass, sometimes. From the camp driveway to a little beyond where those two women I met today have their cabin, the road is either flat or it goes up and down small hills. Just past their cabin, the road starts heading down a long steep grade. On one side of the road, at this point, there is an even steeper drop into a gully, about two hundred feet below the road.

Richard Ebner

As I started driving along towards my new neighbor's cabin, I wasn't at all concerned with the road conditions. I was busy making a mental list of things I wanted to pick up in town. When I reached their cabin, I tooted my horn and reminded myself about the newspaper they wanted. A short time later, I proceeded over the crest of that long steep grade I just told you about.

Something felt a little strange. At first it just seemed that I was traveling a little too fast. I lightly pumped my brakes, nothing happened. I had brakes – but, on the ice, I might as well not have had any, for all the good they did. My speed picked up. I looked to the side of the road and the drop into the gully looked very close indeed. Again, I pumped the brakes and again nothing happened. My speed picked up. I looked to the side of the road and the trees were going past in a blur.

Now, as yet, I wasn't panicky, for I knew that I had the ultimate brake – a four-hundred-pound steel plow on the front of my truck. In the past, I had used the plow to stop the truck on ice, when the brakes wouldn't do it. Keeping this in mind, I tried the brakes one last time – nothing. My speed picked up, time to lower the plow blade. I lowered the blade slowly and as soon as it made contact with the ice, the back of my truck decided it wanted to go first.

I went into an uncontrollable spin. Steering meant nothing. I

Staying Stoned

felt sure I was going to hit the ice-packed snow bank, flip over, and go tumbling into the gully, smashing into trees. Fortunately, this did not happen, or this would have been a very short book. After about a hundred feet of spinning, the plow blade dug into the snow bank, stopping my truck, like an anchor stops a ship.

I was quite shaken. Little did I know that my troubles were not over. From inside the cab, it looked as though I was stuck in the snow bank, but I tried backing up anyway. That was useless. Time to get a shovel from the back of my truck, I thought! When I stepped out, I fell flat on my face and slid about ten feet down the road. Getting back up was no easy task.

I had to crawl up the road until I reached the truck again. And then, I had to hold on to the side of it to stand up. If anyone had been watching me, it must have looked like a scene from a Charlie Chaplin movie or the Three Stooges minus two. I shuffled my way to the rear of my truck and got a shovel.

After about twenty minutes of shoveling, during which I fell down several more times, I was ready to try backing up again. I was ready but my truck was not. Since my truck was sitting sideways in the road, a new concern began to come to me – what if someone else was fool enough to try and drive into town, in this freezing nightmare! I decided I must remove my truck from blocking the road, even if I could not get it unstuck. I attached a chain to the truck's tow hitch and another chain to a large tree, by the side of the road. Then, using a device called a "come-a-long," I was able to winch the back end of my truck out of the road.

Just as I was about to unhitch the chains and the come-a-along, I was alerted to the sound of another car approaching from over the top of the hill. From the sound of the tires, on the ice-covered road, the car was traveling pretty fast for the weather conditions. Soon, I was able to see that the car was not a car at all, but another four-wheel drive truck tooling along without a care in the world. The driver noticed my truck and made his attempts at stopping. As his truck slid from one side of the road to the other, I went for cover behind the largest tree I could find.

Peeking out behind the tree I could see the look of terror on the driver's face. He was learning what I had just learned twenty minutes earlier, that our four-wheel drive vehicles are not invincible. Somehow, he gave up his attempts at stopping and he managed to steer his truck through the narrow space I had just created, between my truck and the snowbank. It was really an amazing driving feat and if I ever see him again, I will tell him. As it was, I don't know when he did finally stop, if ever. I watched him continue his journey down the hill and all future attempts at stopping failed. Every few seconds, his brake lights would go on and off, but his truck just kept on going.

Staying Stoned

When my fellow traveler was finally out of sight, I returned to the task of getting my truck unstuck. Looking around in the bed, for something to improve my truck's traction, I found a couple of Misty's extra dog chains. Using them, I fashioned a rather crude set of tire chains. These chains proved to be the solution.

The only problem left now, was how to get home safely. Turning around in the road was out of the question. So, I decided to continue down the hill. This time, I placed the tip of the plow into the snowbank and plowed my way down the hill. That worked nicely to control my speed and to improve steering. Once I reached the paved road, I didn't have any more trouble getting into town. That road had been sanded and salted. In town, I found out the reason Lime Kiln road had not been sanded. The sander could not make it up the hill.

The ride back was much better. My truck was able to make it up the hill okay, but I remained very nervous until I was back inside my cabin. Right now, I don't care if I ever go out again. I may stay inside until the spring thaw. Oh yes, I did manage to get my neighbor's newspaper for them, but I hardly think it was worth the trouble.

Richard Ebner

Monday, January 22
11:15 AM

Today has started out on a more peaceful note than yesterday and I am liking it this way. The freezing rain has stopped, but the trees keep creaking under the strain of holding up their ice-covered branches. The seriousness of almost losing my truck didn't really strike me until this morning. Had my truck been smashed out of all usefulness, it most likely would have ended this attempt at writing. Today at breakfast, I sat thinking about how dependent I am on that half-ton pick-up of mine. Without it, no more hauling wood around, no more plowing, and no more dragging felled trees out of the woods. I have gained great respect for ice-covered roads, especially the hilly ones around here.

What looks human, can hover in midair, and thinks it is a humming bird? Give up? A helicopter pilot on acid.

Two rabbit hunters showed up at the camp just now, with three beagles in the back of their Jeep. We talked for a few minutes and they asked me if I minded them hunting here. This was not an easy question for me to answer. Personally, I do not like to hunt. However, if a someone eats what they kill, I don't know if that is morally wrong. Can it be any more morally wrong than raising animals to be slaughtered, and then us buying packaged meat at the supermarket?

My main objection to letting these two men hunt here is that I don't want the animals to feel threatened. If I let hunters on the property, I am afraid I will never get to see any of the wild animals that live around here. Never get to see them alive anyway. At the same time, I have heard that if you ban hunters from your property, you can have trouble with them. I don't want my mailbox shot full of holes by angry, frustrated, want-a-be hunters. So, I told them they could hunt here, but I also told them that there are a pair of pet rabbits running loose on the property and that if they shot them by accident, I would be very mad. Then I adjusted my holster. I guess the idea of trying to tell the difference between loose pet rabbits and loose wild rabbits made them decide to hunt elsewhere. Anyway, they left.

High winds and more snow has been predicted for tonight.

Wednesday, January 24
4:30 PM

On the way into town to do my laundry, I saw those two rabbit hunters by the side of the road. I stopped and asked if they had gotten any rabbits. It seems they didn't have any luck with the rabbits. But, they did manage to lose one of their beagles, or it lost them. I guess the rabbits had all the luck today.

Thursday, January 25
2:00 AM

While I was talking to my brother on the phone earlier, one of those rabbit hunters came to the door. That was about ten o'clock. His beagle hadn't returned and he asked me if I would take it in, if the dog came to my cabin. He needn't have asked, I couldn't refuse any animal shelter for a night, if they needed or wanted it. In fact, I think it would make for a nice adventure to go out and look for the little lost creature, right now. Not that I am overly fond of beagles. My tastes tend to run toward the slightly larger breads. But, a lost dog is a lost dog and I do love to play the role of rescuer.

Thursday, January 25
11:00 AM
The girl with the single maraca

Do you realize the significance of this date for me? Being the twenty-fifth means that it is one month that I have been here. This also means that I have not consumed anything on the following list; acid, alcohol, cocaine, marijuana, mescaline, psychedelic mushrooms, nicotine, or speed. When I left for Lime Kiln, my father predicted that I would be back in two weeks. Sorry Dad, but this may be the first project in my life that I actually finish.

It has occurred to me that, with all my talk about how much I love taking drugs, you might have gotten the impression that I was born with a joint in my mouth. This is not true. Although, there have been times this past month when I felt I would like to smoke a joint. I have found it more difficult to stop smoking cigarettes than pot.

There was a time in my life, when I thought I would never be a dope smoker. In fact, I didn't smoke my first joint until I was sixteen, rather late in life by today's standards. Prior to 1969, I thought that alcohol was the thing to do and that smoking marijuana was dumb.

A friend of mine kept working on me to try grass, and I kept arguing that booze was better. It was easier to get, cost less, and if you got caught with it, there was no big deal. He kept saying that smoking grass gave you a better high and never left you with a hangover.

The arguments continued until one summer day in Boston. This friend, whom I will call Rob, and I were walking around Boston Common for lack of anything better to do. When we returned to my car, that was parked alongside the common, a young black boy came up to Rob and asked him if he wanted to buy some grass. I don't know how he knew that Rob was the one to ask. Rob said he was interested and the young pot dealer told him that if we gave him a ride back to his house, he would sell us an ounce of pot for twelve dollars. Rob told me this was a good price for an ounce. Back then, ounces of grass usually sold for fifteen to twenty dollars, depending on how good it was and who sold it to you. I told Rob that I didn't care how good a bargain it was, I didn't want any. Rob practically begged me to just drive him and he would buy the pot himself. I yielded to the pressure.

When we were all on the road, I asked the Black boy in my back seat where he lived. "Roxbury," he replied. Now if you are a nice suburban white boy from Chelmsford, you know that you are never supposed to go to Roxbury. It just wasn't done, not back then, anyway. Even though I was a liberal teenager who was shocked when Martin Luther King Jr. was assassinated the year before, Roxbury was still off limits.

After all, a white person could get killed down there, wherever it was. For me, this was only the second black person I had ever spoken to in my life. The first was a black woman that came into the drugstore, where I worked. I remember telling myself, to just act natural, when she came up to my cash register.

Staying Stoned

Back then, if you asked me if I was prejudiced I would certainly have said no. I would even have gone on to tell you how much I supported the Civil Rights Movement – although, I never did anything to really support it. You just don't meet too many black people in Chelmsford. Fortunately, when I worked for P.B. Inc., in Lowell, I had the opportunity to get to know many blacks. Remind me later, to tell you more about that, and my awakening to my own prejudices.

For now, let's get back to our trip to Roxbury. Neither Rob or I had any idea where Roxbury was. I just knew that it was a part of Boston where I was afraid to go. We drove along with our young black passenger telling me when to turn right and when to turn left. As we got closer, I noticed a change in the proportions of blacks to whites on the streets. Soon, nearly everyone I saw was black. I wanted to lock my door but I was afraid the kid in the back seat would notice. You don't want to let blacks know you are afraid of them. There is no telling what they will do.

Eventually, we stopped in front of a brown brick apartment building that the boy said was his home. As soon as he was out of the car, I locked my doors. It seemed like hours before he returned. I kept telling Rob that if he didn't come back soon, I was taking off. When the boy did return, he handed Rob a plastic bag of pot, and Rob gave the boy twelve bucks. We left without asking any directions of how to get out of Roxbury.

I don't know how we did get out of Roxbury that day. We just kept driving until we recognized something. Once we were in familiar territory, I began to worry about cops. In 1969, in Massachusetts, you could be busted for just being in the presence of marijuana. Every time I saw a police car, I felt sure we were going to be stopped and that they would find the grass. Rob would be arrested for the grass, and I would be arrested for aiding and abetting. My first experience with marijuana paranoia.

Somehow, we made it back to my parent's house without getting busted. Rob started cleaning the sticks and seeds out of his new purchase. This was the first time I had seen an ounce of grass close up. Although I was against smoking marijuana, I was interested in how it was done. I remember making wise cracks about how much easier it was to just open a can of beer and chug it down. All the sifting, and separating of seeds, that Rob had to do seemed silly to me. I wondered why they called it an ounce, since when you got done cleaning it, there was much less than an ounce.

After Rob finished cleaning the grass, he rolled a joint and he resumed his attempt at getting me to smoke. I resisted. Rob kept pressuring me. It seemed so important that I should smoke with him, that at some point, I gave in to it. I don't know if it was because, after all the trouble I went through to help him get the stuff, it seemed silly not to try some, now that it was here in front of me. Or, if it was because of how important it was to my friend, or if I was just a little curious about this weed thing, that was causing so much controversy. Maybe, it was a little of all three.

Anyway, Rob lit the joint, took a hit, and handed it to me. I was not a smoker, of any kind, at that time. So, I had some trouble getting the smoke down into my lungs, where Rob said I wanted it. After some instructions, and a few attempts at holding the smoke in, it felt like my lungs were expanding even though I had stopped breathing in air. I blew the smoke out in one big gasp, where upon, I started coughing violently. Rob told me that this was a sign of pot with a high resin content. He said, "This must be really good shit!" If this was what good shit did to you, I hoped I never came across any bad shit. I was told to take smaller hits and to mix the smoke with air, as I inhaled. This was supposed to make me cough less. Maybe it did, I really don't remember.

All I do remember from this, my first experience at smoking pot, was that I got a sore throat and a rather nasty headache. Rob said he got high from the stuff, but I think he just wanted to so badly, that he believed he did. I come to this conclusion because Rob eventually threw this particular source of pot away, before finishing it. That is something rarely done by a pot smoker with an ounce of, "Really good shit."

Right after this first experience with marijuana, I felt that I need never try it again. I really believed this was to be my first and last use. After all, who wants to smoke something who's only effects were to give you a sore throat and a headache? Before that summer was over however, I had another experience with pot that changed everything.

One August night, late that summer, I was invited to a party by a different friend of mine. When I arrived at the party late, I learned that he had left early. Too embarrassed to leave right away, I decided to stay for a while and see what the party was like. Most of the activity was taking place in a large room, with several chairs and two couches. All the couches and chairs were filled to capacity and many more people were standing around in a circle. At the center of the circle and at the center of attraction, were three people playing musical instruments. A guitar, a flute, and a bass.

Other people were banging on table tops and blowing into bottles. Everyone seemed very involved in the music making, music making that was mostly improvisational, and sounded awful to me. I found a spot that was out of the way, where I could lean up against a wall, and just watch. My body was tense, rigid in fact. I was the only one in the room who was not moving to the music. I felt very much out of place. Not knowing anyone there did not help.

Not far from me was a young woman playing a single maraca. I liked the way she looked and I found myself concentrating on her, and screening out the rest of the party. She looked over in my direction and smiled at me. I smiled back but could not think of anything to say in order to start a conversation. After a while, I noticed that people were passing joints around the room. Why I never smelled the pot before this, I don't know, maybe I was too nervous to notice.

When the joint had made its way around the room to the girl with the single maraca, I began to wonder if I should try some. I was interested in this girl and was afraid that if I refused to smoke, she might not be interested in me. She took a deep hit and passed the joint to me. Without a moment's hesitation, I took an equally deep hit from the joint, and passed it on. Soon another joint came around the room, in the other direction, and then another and another.

I don't know when I first became aware that I was high, but at some point, I realized that I was not standing still anymore. Instead I was bopping along to the music and the music sounded much better to me. Soon the girl with the single maraca and I were giggling, and talking to each other. Now I had plenty of things to say!

I stayed at the party for a long time that night, only walking home at almost dawn. On my way home, I felt very strange, very happy, although I did not know why at the time. Life seemed so new. Even the street I lived on seemed new to me, despite having walked it many times. The sound of dogs barking in the neighborhood was pleasant to me. I was at peace with the world.

As I lay in bed that morning and reflected on the party, the music, the girl with the single maraca, and the marijuana, I felt that I had found a new friend. No, not the girl, for I never even got her name. Pot was my new friend. Booze had never made me feel this way and I liked the way I was feeling. I did not know when, but, I knew I would smoke grass again, soon.

Friday, January 26
9:30 PM

Yesterday at 2:00 AM, I was about to go on a search for a little lost beagle, remember? Well the search turned up nothing, although, Misty loved the opportunity to play bloodhound for a while. She and I combed the reservoir road for about two hours. They call it a road, even though it hardly resembles one, anymore. Most of the road is overgrown with brush, and many large trees have fallen across it. More of an unkempt trail at best.

Staying Stoned

Hunting beagles, that have been hunting rabbits, is not easy. It seems that the little beagles run everywhere the little rabbits go. Fortunately for me, Misty did all the tracking and I was able to concentrate on just walking. A job that was not easy in itself. Since the snow was heavily encrusted from the ice-storm the other day, I was not able to use my newly borrowed snowshoes. Also, the crust on the top of the snow was not quite strong enough to support my weight. This meant that just as I would establish my footing, the crust would give way, often times causing me to trip and fall. The things I will do for little lost animals. Early on in our search, Misty picked up the beagle's tracks, which followed very closely to a set of rabbit tracks.

Something is scratching at the front and back doors, right now. One something could be Misty. I wonder what the other something might be? A beagle, perhaps!

Saturday, January 27
Morning

Sorry to leave you hanging all night and to go to bed without telling what was at the door. I became a bit distracted, when I opened the front door last night. If you remember, something was scratching at both doors. I opened the front door slowly, and carefully, with flashlight in hand. There is no light on the front porch. Expecting to find either Misty or a beagle, I was most surprised to see a raccoon hanging on the screen door, that had been left half open.

Now I know that you might be a little skeptical of this report, considering my previous tales of beavers, that turned out to be muskrats. I assure you, I do know what a raccoon looks like. In fact, the owners of Lime Kiln had some pet raccoons, pet skunks, and even a pet porcupine. I had plenty of opportunities to pet them, have them on my lap, and get to know what they look like. I am somewhat of a dog whisperer, but I only wish I could have a better understanding of some of the less domesticate creatures on this earth.

Hanging there, on my screen door, two feet in front of me, was my raccoon. I was tempted to invite him in for tea or something, when Misty came bounding around from the back yard. The raccoon was attempting to climb down, as Misty bolted into the kitchen, without even noticing what was happening. She turned around and suddenly noticed that we had company. I kept Misty at bay, with one leg and a foot, as I watched the raccoon climb down and scamper into the woods.

I remember now that I had put some of Misty's dog food out on the porch in a frying pan, in case the little beagle came around, while Misty and I were out looking for him. Maybe that is what attracted the raccoon. If he is spotted again, I will bring you a live report.

Sunday, January 28
6:45 AM

The raccoon never returned last night, or if he did, I never heard him. This morning, I awoke to the sound of a quail, that had flown inside the screened-in porch out back, and could not find his way out. After guiding the noisy bird off the porch, I noticed the snow. Since the radio had only predicted flurries, I was surprised to find another three to four inches, on the ground, and more on its way down through the sky. Once again, firewood is diminished, and roads need plowing.

Monday, January 29
2:00 AM

As I got up just now, to let Misty out to relieve herself, I was witness to a bit of excitement. Upon opening the front door, Misty burst past me, barking and chasing something. I quickly stuck just my head out the door to see what was up. I wasn't dressed for going outside. The raccoon is, "What was up!" Misty had treed our raccoon friend. It would seem that Misty did not like her food being eaten by him or her. I don't know how I will ever be able to observe any wild animals, for very long, with Misty's constant protectiveness.

Monday, January 29
10:00 AM
Snow, splinters, quails, and puppy dog tails

The cabin needs a good sweeping today. There are wood chips everywhere. One thing about heating with wood is that you need to be tolerant of splinters. So, bad as the splinter problem is around here, it has inspired another poem:

> I think I will someday see
> A splinter as big as a tree.
> Or at least if all combined,
> Enough for a stately pine.
> There are splinters in my feet.
> There are splinters in my seat.
> And because of this I find
> A splinter in my behind.
> Everywhere that I may walk,
> In this house of which I talk,

Splinters lie all around, on the ground
And in my socks, they be found.

Tuesday, January 30

It is snowing again. So, what's new? It has been snowing since Sunday, I think. Reports are that it will snow through Wednesday.

Wednesday, January 31
10:00 PM

Update on the snow report. Wednesday is almost over and the snow keeps coming down, not very fast, about four inches per day. Since it has been snowing from Sunday on, there is about sixteen inches of new snow. Latest predications are that it will continue to snow at least until tomorrow night. Meteorologists have an interesting, but difficult job. And, unlike carpenters, you can never hold them accountable for making mistakes.

After getting my truck stuck for the third time today, I have given up trying to plow for now. I fear I will not be able to plow, all the roads, inside the camp, anymore. Besides providing an easy place to walk, having the roads plowed have made access to firewood easier. I am sure going to miss being able to drive right up to the trees I want to cut down. Maybe, in the light of day, tomorrow, I can find a way to plow some of them, without getting stuck.

Just clearing the road into the camp, and a work area, around my cabin, I spent about four hours today. Glad I didn't have to do it with a shovel. Because the road into the camp is narrow, and lined with trees, on both sides, after a few snow storms, the banks won't hold any more snow. This means I must plow the snow all the way out to Lime Kiln road, and push it up onto the banks that the town plow has made. I'm just glad I haven't gotten stuck while doing that. As you know, the last time my truck was blocking the road it almost ended in disaster.

It also occurs to me, that I should probably shovel some snow off of the roofs. I can only see the tops, of the chimneys now. I wouldn't want my cabin or the owner's house to collapse on my watch.

CHAPTER III

February, 1979

Thursday, February 1
10:00 PM
Pot, sex, and the older woman

It was wise of me to stop plowing when I got stuck, for the third time, last night. When I went out to my truck this morning, I was amazed at how completely stuck I had gotten. There was snow packed up under the truck, for its entire length. Two hours of shoveling finally freed it, and I was able to plow most of the roads in the camp today.

Tonight, is one of those blustery, gusty-winded nights, when having any shelter at all is greatly appreciated. It makes me feel especially cozy, to be sitting here, in front of my small wood stove, and with my dog curled up on the old overstuffed chair beside me. And you of course, in the form of my magnetic tape recorder friend.

Do you ever think about sex? Silly question – I know I do, although not as much perhaps as I did when I was sixteen. Back then, I thought about it a lot. Even before then, when I hadn't had a sexual experience, with another person yet, sex was often on my mind. I wondered what it would be like, and most of all, I wondered when I would get my chance. When and where would I find a girl who was willing, or if not willing, at least one who could be talked into the idea? Please note, I said 'talked', not forced. If you are a young dude who hasn't had sex yet, you might start the conversation with any potential partner, by reading the instructions on a box of condoms together. Just a thought.

Many a night I spent driving around, in my car, with my friends, looking for sex. As if you could find it out on the road, if you were just lucky enough to be on the right street, at the right time. Of course, you can find sex on certain streets, in almost any city, if you want to pay for it. But a prostitute is out of the question, for most of us at sixteen.

In some ways, a young man who feels he must have sex at that age might be better off going to a prostitute, rather than chasing around girls his own age, and trying to get in their pants. I know what I have just said may seem shocking to some people. However, it could help solve many problems. Problems like teenage pregnancy or emotional problems caused by a girl having sex before she is ready.

Yes, boys too can have emotional problems from having sex before they are ready as well. But, for the most part, boys don't take sex as seriously as girls. Maybe because society encourages young men to have sex. For a boy, it is a sign of manhood to have had sex early. A girl who tries it is considered a slut, or has loose morals.

The main reason that boys, and men too, don't take sex as seriously as girls and women do, is because they know they can't get pregnant. This is one of the reasons, I think, it may be better if young men went to a prostitute, instead of their girlfriends, to relieve their sexual desires. Of course, it might be better still, if they were able to wait, until both their sexual maturity and their emotional maturity were equally developed.

I wish I had been able to wait. Easy for me to say now. Back then, it seemed so important for me to score. That all important desire, for me to have sex, with a girl, caused me to ruin, what could have been my first meaningful relationship, with a person of the opposite sex. A girl whom I liked very much, and whom I think liked me, at the time, was lost to me, as soon as we had sex.

After several weeks of coercing, I managed to get her alone

in my bedroom one day, when no one else was home at my parent's house. By putting all kinds of guilt trips on her, and by being very manipulative, I was able to get her to agree to have sex with me. Well, she just let me do it. Since neither of us had any experience at it, the whole encounter was very awkward and I am sure, not very satisfying for her. Once I took her home, we didn't see much of each other anymore. We were both too embarrassed. I had traded a nice developing friendship, for a thirty-second chance to score.

The idea of a relationship for a teenage girl seems to be more of an emotional and spiritual nature, than of a physical one. Girls like to cuddle and neck, and be held. I think it makes them feel loved and wanted and romantic. Boys, on the other hand, like to cuddle, neck, and be romantic, because it puts them within striking range. The more you hug and hold a girl, which is what she wants, the better your chances of getting what you want, to go all-the-way.

Well, from my experience, many times, all-the-way, is not as far as I thought it would be. That is, once you have gone there, so what? Often times, the things you have to sacrifice, on the way there, aren't worth the pay-off, once you get there. When I speak of sacrifice, I am not speaking in religious terms, like sacrificing one's virginity. I mean honesty, mutual respect, trust, and most of all, caring.

The boy who tells a girl, that if she loved him, she would make it with him, no matter how it would make her feel, isn't being very loving towards the girl. It is a dishonest manipulation of the girl's feelings, and further, shows that the boy is not ready to enter into a serious sexual relationship. I know because I have been there. Bells should go off in a girl's head, when she hears this kind of line from a boy, "I am really in pain down there, and if we don't do it soon I could be permanently disabled." The girl might try responding to this by saying: "If you loved me you would not pressure me into doing something that I am not ready to do, or I might become permanently disabled."

The game playing involved in teenage sexual encounters tends to destroy the good loving feelings that can arise out of a mature healthy sexual relationship. That is not to say, being an adult makes a person immune to game-playing, or from manipulation. Some of the worst manipulators of sex are adults. When you are a teenager, though, you are in a period of life when you are adjusting to so many new stressors and emotional feelings, that the added burden of a sexual encounter can be very confusing, and often, quite frightening.

Another popular form of sexual manipulation is the seduction. Adults like to use alcohol for this. As a late teenager, I was prone to use pot to try and seduce girls, especially when I was trying to have sex with no emotional involvement. If I found out that a certain girl liked to smoke grass and that she was willing to smoke alone with me, I took it as a signal that she was also willing to have sex with me.

That was not always the case. Sometimes the girl just liked to get high and talk. For me though, this would not be enough. I would keep trying to turn the moment into a sexual experience. This type of behavior not only destroyed many potential relationships with girls, it also caused many of my male friends not to trust me around their girlfriends.

With so much of society's adult world telling us, through television, movies, and in advertising, that you are not a real person unless you are sexually active, it is little wonder that when you are a teenager, you want to become sexually involved, as soon as you can. Perhaps, I am already too old to really understand, what being a young teenager is like? I think not.

I feel better able to relate to the teenagers, of the world, than to the so-called adults, with all their hatred and hypocrisy. Adults say that drugs are bad and then continue to kill themselves with alcohol. Or, adults tell kids not to fight, but are willing to have those same kids die in wars over oil and property. Maybe this is part of why I have continued to do drugs and have never fit into the adult world.

If you are the kind of person who reads the headings, at the top of the page, you may have noticed that, so far, I have talked about two of the subjects listed, pot and sex. That's right, I am now going to talk about older women. How could you tell?

In order to tell this next story of my past, properly, I should start when I was ten, a time when all women were older women. My parents and I were in New York City, for the wedding of a long-time friend of theirs. Both of the to-be-weds had been married before, and the woman of the two, as this was a conventional male/female marriage, had a daughter from her previous marriage. This daughter's name was Katherine, probably still is for that matter.

Anyway, Katherine was thirteen or fourteen, at the time, and not too happy with the idea of her mother remarrying. In order to help drive home the point, Katie, as she liked to be called, and I played a few practical jokes on mother dearest. We started with substituting salt for the sugar, in the sugar bowl, and ended with placing a squeaky toy under her mother's pillow.

These were silly, dumb, immature things to do, in the opinion of the adults. For Katie and me though, all the sneaking around and tension of trying not to get caught, gave us a sense of comradeship. A feeling that allowed us to become friends quickly. From that weekend onward, I had a crush on Katie, that lasted until I was seventeen.

I saw Katie two more times, before I turned seventeen – once when I was in New York City with my mother, for a week, and once when Katie came to stay with us for a few days, at my parent's house, in Chelmsford, Mass. Both times were less than perfect meetings, as far as I was concerned.

I still had that boyhood crush, when I returned to the city, with my mother. It left me totally unprepared for the idea of Katie having a boyfriend, that wasn't me. I retaliated by keeping her boyfriend as busy as possible, showing me around the city. If I couldn't have Katie to myself, at least I could keep her away from others. Needless to say, my plan didn't help deepen her feelings for me. Don't you just hate it when people say, "Needless to say," and then they go ahead and say it anyway?

The next meeting was even more devastating, for me. I was ecstatic, when I first learned Katie was coming to stay with us, for three or four days. Most of the first day went great. My brother drove Katie, my mother, and me, around in his convertible. We were showing Katie the sights. Sometime during the day, there was talk of going to a drive-in movie, later that night. At the time, I thought the idea was great. Only later, when I learned the plans did not include me, did I think it was a stupid idea.

I had a hard time understanding why Katie, now sixteen years old, would rather go to a movie, with my eighteen-year-old brother, than thirteen-year-old me. I flipped out! Jumping on my ten-speed, I tore down the driveway and didn't come home until after midnight. Undaunted, my brother and Katie went to the movies – so much for my being dramatic.

I have given you this background stuff, as we writers call it, so that you can appreciate where I was coming from, when I was to meet Katie once more, after my seventeenth birthday. Again, in the company of my mother, but this time, in my own convertible, and with me driving, we headed for New York, upstate New York, that is.

Katie's mother and stepfather owned a small house on Lake Carmel, which they used as a retreat, from their high-pressure jobs, in Manhattan. My mother and I were invited to spend this particular weekend, out at the lake with them. Well, that's not quite true. My mother was invited. I sort of invited myself, when I learned that Katie would be there, without a male companion.

Being seventeen now, having my driver's license and my own car, I felt I was a man. Feeling I was a man, and knowing Katie was without one, for the moment, I felt sure she would be interested in me. She wasn't! Not that she wasn't nice to me, she was very nice. It's just that I wanted more of a boy/girl relationship, if you know what I mean. Oh, all right... I wanted to get laid.

That was not to be, not with Katie at any rate. We did go out together, and any unsuspecting stranger would have thought us, to be a couple. The time spent alone together was awkward though. I had the distinct feeling that she was only being a polite hostess. If the time was awkward for me, it must have been even more so, for her.

After going out to a local bar, Friday night, and a carnival Saturday afternoon, my polite hostess found a way to divert my attention. She called a girlfriend of hers, who was home from the same college that she went to, in Colorado. The two of them talked on the phone for a while, and then made arrangements for the three of us to meet and go out Saturday night. The plan was for Katie and I to drive to her friend's house, about thirty miles north of Carmel, and then go out to a local bar, up there.

I had mixed feelings about the meeting at first. I felt it was clearly an attempt to pass me off. Since things were not exactly going great between Katie and myself, there didn't seem to be any better options. Visions of a fat, ugly girl, that nobody wanted, and a boring evening, were conjured up in my head. And it is strange that I thought that way. Back in high school, I tended to be more attracted to the girls that might be a bit heavier, and not as stunning as the cheerleader types. Most of those girls were more interesting – more real!

We drove up to the friend's house, in my car, and Katie

Staying Stoned

talked about her college girlfriend, during the entire ride. This, I thought, was a bad sign. The bigger the build-up and the harder the sell, the more the dog of a girl was to be expected. If you are thinking that I was a bit of a chauvinist, in those days – you're right! However, for forty-five minutes, I was subjected to a sibilant succession of superjacent superlatives. In other words, I was told she was wonderful in all respects. Everything from what a great swimmer she was to how well she could drive a pick-up truck was shared. I didn't let any of it impress me.

Eventually we arrived at Katie's friend's house. As we pulled into the driveway, we were met by a barking dog. No, not my blind date, a real canine-type dog. Sorry about that, Mr. Sexist Pig keeps creeping back up every now and then, like a recurring disease. Shortly after the dog, a young, well-tanned woman, with short blonde hair, emerged from the house at the top of the driveway. As she crossed in front of my car, the headlights focused my attention on her shape. She had all the right curves in all the right places.

Call it love at first sight. Call it, a youthful infatuation, with a somewhat older woman. Or, call it a chemical interaction reaction – but something hit me, when I was introduced to this woman.

"Lisa, this is Theo. Theo, this is Lisa." Katie said.

Wham! I was a speechless, adolescent jelly-fish, for the rest

123

of the night. Most of my responses were limited to some awkward head-bobbing. I began to feel that Lisa must have been thinking that I was mentally challenged by my strange behavior. If I were to judge the evening, by what was said or done, it wouldn't rate very high. It was just a few hours, in a night long ago, spent drinking beer, and listening to the juke box, in a little redneck bar, in upstate New York.

All during the evening a very large truck driver, who was quite at home in this bar, kept buying us drinks and dancing with Lisa. There wasn't much I could do, except sit there drinking my beer and wishing I was older. Even being seventeen and having a driver's license and my own convertible, didn't seem to be enough. How come so much of our youth is spent wishing we were older? Then, when we get older, we blame our age for keeping us from doing the things we want to do.

As the night wore on, I began to get panicky. Soon, the evening would be over and Katie and I would return to Carmel, leaving Lisa behind, forever. Unless I acted quickly, to come up with a plan to see her again, that would be the last of my beautiful, blonde, blind date. I do love euphonious alliteration, don't you? And a good thesaurus helps.

How could I interest Lisa in seeing me again? Me, a poor, humble, seemingly stupid teenage boy from Massachusetts. I hadn't said more than a dozen words, all evening. Still, something in me had to ask her, if I could come out to New York and see her again. It never seemed like the right time. If she wasn't dancing, with the redneck truck driver, she was listening to him tell jokes, at our table. He was such a man's man, and such an asshole – I thought at the time. Of course, now I can admit he was probably no more of an asshole than me – just more experienced.

Whenever I was relatively alone, with Lisa, my courage to ask her delayed, until we were alone no longer. During the ride back to Lisa's house, I composed a hundred different ways to ask for another meeting, but none of them seemed worthy of repeating aloud. I knew that soon we would be parting. My desperate need for more contact, with this person, would be unattainable, if I didn't say something. It appeared very much unattainable anyway.

At the very last moment, when we were again in Lisa's driveway, and while the two women were still saying good-bye, something blurted out of me.

"I must see you again," was all I could say. How original. Huh?

Maybe it was the emotion in my voice. Or maybe it was just the compassionate nature of this woman, that caused her to turn and kiss me affectionately on my cheek. Then Lisa said the only words, that I heard clearly, all night, "That would be nice."

The next three weeks were spent scheming how to make my rendezvous come true. There were all sorts of details to work out. First, I would need a private place to stay. Someplace supportive of seduction. Since Lisa had said yes to seeing me again, I thought I was real hot stuff. After all, if she wanted to see me, even though I hadn't said much of anything, I must have been overflowing, with good old animal magnetism. Right? Well, regardless of my sexual attractiveness, I would need a spot to bed down. It was a four-hour drive, from my parent's house, in Massachusetts, to the Carmel area of New York. Kind of a long drive for just an evening's date.

I remembered noticing that Katie's folk's house on the lake was in desperate need of repainting. A plan came to mind. I got in touch with Katie's dad and offered to paint the house, in exchange for letting me stay there by myself for a week. The plan worked – he agreed.

Next, I needed to get in touch with Lisa, to let her know, when I would be in town again, as they say. As who says? Isn't that a dumb expression? Anyway, I reached for a small piece of paper in my wallet that had Lisa's phone number on it. In those days, I always kept phone numbers of prospective girlfriends in my wallet, for safe keeping and quick reference. Unfortunately, I grabbed the wrong little piece of paper at first, and started to make a person-to-person call, to the gas station downtown. I caught myself before the call was complete, however. Person-to-person was a little trick I used, when I didn't want to explain to a girl's parents, who I was or what I wanted, with their daughter. Let the operator do the talking. This time, Lisa answered the phone herself.

'Lisa, I'll be in town on the tenth. So, drop what you're doing and get ready. And, don't be late,' I said. I didn't really say any of that. Already, this story is taking longer to tell than I wanted. Cutting to the chase, Lisa agreed to see me

Now that I had a place to stay and a real live female to stay with me, all I needed was some good grass, I thought. I wasn't close to my friend, Guru, yet. So, I had to rely on another friend for my supply of drugs. In order to seduce a twenty-one-year old, college woman, I figured I better have plenty of really good weed, none of that cheap shit, dirt weed. An operation of this magnitude required nothing less than Gold. Not being able to afford a full once, I settled for a dime bag. Since Lisa told me that she could only get one day off, from work, she was a lifeguard during the summer, I guessed that a dime bag might be enough. I wasn't altogether sure.

During the next two weeks, before I left for New York, I was a mister wonderful, around the house. I mowed the lawn, without complaints and took out the trash, without being told. I even looked forward to doing the dishes. Anything that would keep me busy and help make the time pass more quickly. Two weeks and two days, after that phone call to Lisa, I packed my car and headed for the house by the lake.

I arrived at around noon. There was only one road in and out of Lake Carmel. That road circled around the lake and exited where it started from. The house where I'd be staying was the fifth one in on the right. All along the road were a mixture of pine trees, oaks and a few maples.

For the next two days, I buried myself in the work of painting the house. Lisa was due to come down and stay with me, on Tuesday night, and maybe Wednesday. That meant I had two days and three nights to kill, before she would be there. I scraped and painted and scraped and painted, in an attempt to exhaust myself each day, so that I could get to sleep each night. And while the pine trees smelled great, and provided shade, they also left a lot of pine pitch to be cleaned off before painting was possible.

Finally, it was Tuesday morning and I greeted the day with tremendous energy, running everywhere, even up ladders, with buckets of white paint. A nosey neighbor stopped by to see what I was doing. She told me that this was a nice quiet community, so I should not play the radio so loud. I had brought my stereo with me. Can't have a seduction if it's not in stereo.

Staying Stoned

I had placed the speakers in an open window so I could have music while working. There was hardly a song I didn't sing along with that day. Knowing how badly I sing, that could have been what was bothering the neighbor, come to think of it.

At about 4:30, I went inside to take a shower and to prepare for my house guest. I rolled four or five joints, from the dime that I had brought with me. Then, I began to wonder if Lisa even smoked. Katie didn't, at least not around me, and Lisa was her friend. If Lisa didn't smoke pot, then my plans to try and get her into bed with me, were in big trouble. I decided not think about it. That decision didn't last long.

I began rationalizing. Even if she didn't sleep with me, we could have a nice time, right? No, not right! Why did it seem so important to score? I wasn't a virgin, although my sexual experiences were greatly limited.

From my first fling at sex, it hardly seemed like something to get so worked up about. I mean the whole thing didn't last more than five minutes, start to finish. That included the time spent taking off our clothes. So, why did it seem so important to have sex with Lisa? A guy drives two hundred miles, scrapes and paints a small, two-story house, for free, and thinks he is the luckiest jerk in the world, because there is a chance that he might spend three minutes in bed with a woman.

My paranoia was interrupted, by the sound of a pick-up

truck, pulling in next to my car. Was it Lisa? As I started for the door, I checked my hair and outfit in the bedroom mirror, just to be sure.

Lisa was pulling a duffel bag, from the cab of her truck, when I reached her. I said, "Hello," and told her that there was a nosey neighbor next door. Once again, I was having trouble saying what I really wanted to say. Somehow, Lisa and I came up with the idea of calling Lisa, Ralph, to try to fool the neighbor into thinking that she was a he. Even though Lisa did have very short hair, with a boyish cut, anyone would have to have been quite blind, not to notice her feminine shape.

I didn't carry Lisa's bag into the house, although I offered. She could have carried the duffel bag, with me in it, I think. From swimming every day, her body was in excellent condition.

We walked up to the house, with me calling her Ralph, every five seconds and her answering, in a deep tone of voice. Once in the house, I started to make us dinner, while Ralph walked through the house looking into every room, and thumbing through my stack of records.

During supper, I continued to wonder about the sleeping arrangements. Even though I had fantasies, about sleeping with Lisa, the idea was by no means a certainty, in my mind. After all, I hardly knew her, and to her, I must have seemed eager. I kept asking as many safe questions as I could, things like, had she ever saved anyone from drowning, and, what courses did she take in college.

Dinner went fairly well. I was very nervous about what I should do afterwards. I was fully prepared to seduce her with my stereo and my pot. A lack of experience, left me, at her mercy instead. All the right equipment, just not enough training, I thought.

I needn't have gotten myself in a tizzy. For soon after supper, Lisa took over for me. She suggested that we go into the living room and put on some music. I put on some Pop/Rock from the mid-sixties. Lisa asked if I had any wine. I told her no, but if she liked, I did have a few joints. That was okay with her. So, we sat on the floor and smoked my first joint.

I don't know just how it came up, but I complained of sore muscles, in my back and shoulders, from painting and scraping. Lisa told me to take my shirt off and lie on my stomach. I did. Two soft but firm hands proceeded to remove the tension from my back and neck. As she messaged my muscles, she spoke to me. The combination of the pot and Lisa's voice, sent me straight to never-never land. Her caring hands didn't stop their wise manipulation of my back and shoulders, until every trace of tightness was gone.

I rolled over, sat up, and just stared into her eyes. She leaned over to me, kissed me, then leaned back to look at me. The warmest, most reassuring smile came over her face. And soon, she returned to kiss me again. This time she gently ran her tongue around my lips, and lightly across my face, barely even making contact. As she did, her breath was blowing softly into my eyes and nose. I could do nothing except sit there.

She took my hands, which were hanging clumsily next to me, and then she placed them up under her sweatshirt. Who was seducing who? Guiding my fingertips, across her nipples, she smiled softly at my innocence.

"Relax," she said in a whisper. "Relax," she repeated, and pressed her body against mine. Then, somewhat forcefully, she pushed me to the floor. I melted into a flat line on the carpet. Lisa sat up again, and removed her shirt. She stayed there for a while, allowing me to view, what I felt, was the most beautiful sight, I had ever seen.

Her nipples were erected, as they starred back into my eyes – and her breasts seemed to be smiling at me as well. Lisa laid down on me again, and those two lovely breasts spread out conforming to my bare chest. I ran my hands across her back.

How soft and supple, her skin, and how firm and strong were her muscles. She kissed me again and again, sometimes letting her tongue wander inside my mouth. After a time, Lisa asked me if I had ever made love to a woman before. I said, "Yes."

Then I added, "But it never lasted very long." Again, she smiled!

We removed the rest of our clothing. I moved above her with the intension of mounting. Then Lisa put both her hands on my chest holding me back. "Slow down," she said. "No need to pull the trigger so fast. I will be with you all night. Neither of us has a plane to catch."

Lisa taught me how to stay in the moment and not race up ahead to try and score some sort of ill-perceived goal. She spoke to me softly as she guided my movements. At some point, we both seemed satisfied. We snuggled. Then Lisa quietly said, "You know, while I enjoy the physicality of sex, it is the spiritual time I cherish most. This time – the afterglow."

The next day, we spent a lot of time just talking. I finished the rest of the grass I had rolled. Pot made the talking easier for me. I wasn't used to talking about my sexuality. Grass seemed to free me from being too guarded, about what I was willing to reveal. If my rendezvous with Lisa, had taken place last week, instead of when it did, I wouldn't have needed drugs for any of those reasons. I don't think Lisa needed them at all, even back then. She just smoked, because she felt it would help me. Grass did seem to help me overcome certain inhibitions or hang-ups.

Richard Ebner

Friday, February 2
7:00 AM

As I think about what I talked about last night, a better idea, than having sex with a prostitute, might be, for each of us to have a someone like Lisa, of our own. That is, males and females alike, might be better off having their first sexual experience, with someone who is more sexually secure, and more emotionally mature than themselves. This does not mean that I am advocating that adults should have sex with children, not at all! If, when young adults feel ready, to explore their sexuality, they could do that exploration with someone who has already done some exploration of their own, it might help make the experience less awkward and more rewarding. Of course, much of the awkwardness of a first sexual experience could be overcome, if parents were able to talk openly, and freely with their children, about their own sexuality.

How can we expect young people to make mature, adult, decisions about sex, if adults are unable to give them the information they need to make those decisions? It is not surprising that most teenagers are unable to talk about birth control, before it is needed. Afterwards it is too late. Adults like to keep sex very mysterious. Television bombards teenagers with the idea of sex and makes them quite aware that sex is all around. It's in the wind.

Ask an adult for some details and many times you can come up a little short. You know, the little nitty-gritty details. Like, does it matter who undresses first? Should the boy share in the responsibility of preventing pregnancy? The idea of two innocent, uninformed people having sex, for the first time together, is a lot like two blind people leading each other through a jungle filled with quicksand and snakes. And still, they do seem to manage to get the right parts in the right places. And too often, one of them gets pregnant. Naturally, always the female.

A lot of what I said here will probably anger most of the members of the clergy. But, that is okay. They are often getting angry for all the wrong reasons. Men of the cloth would like to pretend that kids won't have sex and thus can't get pregnant. Just tell them, it is a sin, and they won't do it. That's bull shit. If you are a priest, a reverend, or a minister, as sure as you have at least one eye that can see, somewhere right now, kids are doing it and a young girl is getting pregnant.

The church is very outspoken about the rights of the unborn child. What about the rights of the children making that child. It does not let you off the hook to say that, it is wrong for teenagers to engage in sex. It may be wrong, or at least, ill-timed

– but, saying it is wrong does not lessen the tragedy of a young girl, with an unwanted child, a young girl, who obviously is not ready to make decisions about her own life, let alone making decisions for another's life.

Would you have wanted me, with all my pre-described drug use, to have raised a child? Don't answer. I wouldn't have done a very good job. Unwittingly, the church, by its stand on abortion and by its emphasis on being married, before exploring sexuality, is contributing to an immoral situation.

The young couple, who believes the only way to redeem themselves, for creating a child out of wedlock, is to get married, only sets the stage for the next generation to repeat their mistakes. How can children be charged with the responsibility of something so precious, as a new, developing human life?

If you let your fourteen-year-old daughter take care of your new born child, while you left town, for eighteen years or so, you would be considered an unfit parent, and your children would be taken from you. This is just what the church is doing, when it agrees to marry the fourteen-year-old, who has gotten pregnant and feels she has no other choices. To me, the priest who performs a marriage, in this case, is more immoral than the two teenagers, who made the mistake of causing a pregnancy.

Staying Stoned

Perhaps abortion is immoral, I don't profess to have the answer. I have tried to imagine what it would be like to be a woman, and pregnant without wanting to be. It's not a very good feeling. Imagine being responsible for another human life, twenty-four hours a day, for nine months. Imagine that human growing inside your body, that hasn't even finished growing itself. Imagine, if you can, that your only choices are to continue with the pregnancy, give birth, and continue to care for that life, until the child turns eighteen. Or, place the child in the care of another through adoption.

If you did your imagining well, it was a scary thought, either way. Now, imagine being able to stop that growth process, before it has become a separate life, while still part of your body. For me, that is still a scary thought, and not something I would take lightly and not necessarily the option I would choose. Then again, I am a male and I can't get pregnant no matter how much I try to imagine.

As I have said, I don't know if abortion is immoral or not. I think, it is a question that only a woman and her God can answer, and priests are not gods, although sometimes they seem to think they are. The question of abortion could become less of an issue, if we could manage to stop so many of the unwanted pregnancies, before they happen. Young people need to have truthful information about sex, before they can decide whether they are ready for it. If you misinform them, they will find out that you lied, and distrust everything you tell them in the future.

The results of misinformation are still having their effects on us, the pot users of the world, and especially in the United States of America. The following quote is taken from the 1957 World Book Encyclopedia: "Marijuana is a narcotic drug... No matter in what form the drug is used, it has undesirable effects on the body. The user loses mental and sometimes physical control of himself and may commit violent crimes. The drug is extremely habit forming and it has no value as a medicine. It has..." Sounds more like the side-effects of alcohol if you ask me. Every incident of domestic violence in my childhood home began with excessive alcohol consumption, and not pot. Oh, and by the way, I am wondering – do you know of any medical uses for alcohol? Maybe rubbing alcohol, which is deliberately made toxic so that you don't drink it. Alcohol should probably be proscribed rather than prescribed for anything.

Another brother of mine, the oldest, and not the gun owner, served six years in the Coast Guard and then contracted Multiple Sclerosis. His neurologists prescribed valium to help with his leg tremors, that kept him up at night. Over time he needed more and more valium, and eventually it stopped working altogether, but the side-effects left him drowsy all day. He asked me if I could get him some marijuana. I did. It worked.

Staying Stoned

Maybe someday grass will be recognized in this country for medical uses. I certainly hope so!

To read that in an encyclopedia today, it almost makes me laugh. This kind of misinformation, from so-called, reliable sources, only helps to intensify the drug problem in this country. When kids see their friends smoking grass and they don't commit violent crimes, they don't lose physical control, and they don't seem to be addicted, those kids begin to doubt everything that authorities tell them about drugs. Similarly, when a young person discovers that he or she does not go blind, after masturbating, that young person has little use for the person, who said it would happen.

Almost as bad, as misinforming young people about sex, is not informing them. As a parent, don't depend on the church, to teach your children, what they need to know about sex. The church has been failing at that task, in ever-increasing numbers, for years. Would you let someone who never drove a car teach your child how to drive? Why be so willing to let a priest teach your child about sex, when he is committed to celibacy? Some priests must be confused about their own sexual feelings, part of the reason they might have become priests. If I were a parent, I'd be rather reluctant to leave my child alone, to ostensibly talk about sex, with a man who is required to suppress his natural desires – I see trouble there. My apologies to all those religions, where celibacy is not a requirement of ordainment. Of course, just because you have had a sexual experience, does not mean that you are an authority on sex, nor does it mean that you necessarily have the capabilities to teach about it.

So, where can a teenager go, to learn about sex, if the church is unwilling to talk about it honestly and the parents are unable? I would like to see human sexual relationships taught, in all the schools. Not just biological sex, but the real joys, sorrows, and uncertainties, of being a human sexual person, should be explored in schools and in the community.

We are willing to be sold everything from toothpaste to perfume by the use of sex. However, when it comes to honest open communication, between each other, we say, "Leave it to the church, or, it's up to the parents, to teach kids about sex." Well, we all share this world. If we want to get a handle on problems, like teenage pregnancy, rape, divorce, alcohol and drug addiction, we better start talking to each other, and we better get educated.

Maybe, I am so obsessed with the problems of youth, because youth is where I feel so many of my problems, and problems of the world, in general, get started. After all, we were all youths once. It seems to me, that we are teaching the kids to have more problems. Did you ever hear someone say: "Life was so much simpler, when I was a child?" If you think life has gotten more complicated, as an adult, imagine how much more complicated it must seem, as a young adult, trying to grow up in today's world.

Teenagers need to be told that it's alright for them not to have sex, or not to take drugs. Not because it is wrong, or immoral, but because it may not be right for them, at this time in their lives. They need to know they have the choice, not to do something, as well as the choice, to do something. Peer pressure is a very difficult thing to go against. Many times, giving in to it is the only way certain teenagers can gain acceptance.

If you can't even talk to your child, you have no chance, of off-setting peer pressure. I remember when I was in high school, some of the kids, who were social out-casts, gained immediate acceptance, as soon as they started smoking grass. Smoking weed is something everyone can do well. You don't need to be an athlete, or have a pretty face, to be a good pot smoker. All you need to do, is be willing to smoke it, and you have friends.

All children need to be able to talk to their parents, without fear of being punished, for what they might be thinking or feeling. With the help and support of understanding adults, many teenagers may be able to find the inner strength necessary, to choose to say no to taking drugs and to choose to wait, for the right time for them to explore their sexuality further.

Friday, February 2
Sitting in a chair and listening to myself talking to you

It is overcast, cold and grey, a typical mid-winter's day. As I listened to the tapes, that I made yesterday, and early this morning, I began to get the feeling that I may have made a number of enemies, from what I said. Be that as it may, I feel what I had to say is so important, that it had to be said, without beating around the bush. And if I pissed off the Catholic Church, this could be good for book sales. Perhaps *Staying Stoned* will be banned – nothing like being banned by Catholics to create a best seller – even if the writing is substandard. It happened for– *The Count of Monte Cristo*, by Alexandre Dumas, *Les Misérables* and *The Hunchback of Notre Dame* –

both by Victor Hugo, *To Kill a Mocking Bird*, by Harper Lee, *Huckleberry Finn*, by Mark Twain, and many, many more ... Of course, none of the books I just mentioned had substandard writing – they were all pretty damn Great! My personal favorite being, *To Kill a Mocking Bird*.

When you have done many things in your life, that you feel have screwed up your life significantly, as I have, there comes a time when you feel you must speak out to try and help others from making similar mistakes with their own lives. So, while I am somewhat concerned if some people were turned off by what I have said, I actually make no apologies.

This weekend, I will have company again, besides You (my tape-recorder), and Misty. My woman friend and my oldest brother are coming to visit me, and see if I am okay. It is about a three-hour drive, for each of them. I am truly touched by their concern.

Speaking of my woman friend, she has her Master's degree in early-childhood education. She teaches high school to students, at a vocational school, to work in the field at daycare centers. One week they travel to a daycare center to work in the trenches, with supervision by my mate. The next week they are in the classroom, with her. She is terrific with her students, and people in general.

An elective, she also teaches is called, Human Relations.

When she presented an idea to administrators about a sex-education curriculum, they approved it, as long as nothing in the title mentioned sex. A tad cowardly of them, but at least they were being responsive to the problem, so good for them!

One of the coolest assignments she devised for her students was the raw egg experiment. She gave each class member a raw egg in its shell and in a small basket with tissue paper. Then, using a felt-tipped marker, they were asked to draw a face on their egg. After that, they were to keep a journal about how well they were protecting their egg. How often they checked on it, turned it, attend to it, was required. Also required, they needed to bring their egg to class with them each day.

At the end of the two-week assignment, very few eggs survived. Some had been dropped in the halls, bumped into on the bus, or crushed by books in their lockers. So, what was the point? It facilitated discussions about what it might be like to have to take care of a baby. Unfortunately, not too many boys signed up for the elective. However, one of the boys from her last class protected his egg well, and turned it in without a crack. Good for him! He might become a great father someday.

So, I think you can understand why I am excited to see my woman friend, who is such a good teacher and just a wonderful human being. And, by the way, no tax dollars were used to buy the eggs, the baskets, or the tissue paper blankets. This teacher paid for everything out of her own funds.

As I get older, I begin to feel more and more, the need for family. But I don't want to be a father. And since my woman already has three children from a former marriage, and because she is seven-teen-years older than me, there doesn't seem to be much pressure about my becoming a dad. I guess I am still infatuated with older women. There is much they have learned, and much they can teach.

When I was younger, growing up at home, our family did a less than perfect job of sticking together and helping each other. This caused me to be very cynical, about the need for families. I became a loner, who blamed most of my problems, on conditions at home.

My oldest brother and I are only now just beginning to get

to know one another, once again. After years of psychological separation, his divorce, and personal growth, on both our parts, we have started to get closer. For years, I have thought of him as my straight brother. He, in turn, probably considered me, to be a bit of a space-shot. In the past, when talking with him about my life and what I wanted to do with it, I felt most of his responses were very negative. He did not seem to want to understand me, and get to know me. I too have been guilty, of only surface interest, in the things that have affected his life.

Whether it is the time of life and/or the substance of what I am trying to do up here, or both, and a thousand other subtle reasons, things are much better between us. The negative disinterest has been replaced by a positive, loving, encouragement. My stopping the daily, and sometimes, constant use of pot must have had some effect on improving our relationship. It was something I know that bothered him, although, he never talked to me about directly.

I remember one day, a long time ago, when I was still living in my parent's house. He was not living there then. Big brother, came over to the house to wash his car. My other brother and I played a cruel, and childish, joke on him. Knowing how he felt about smoking grass at the time, as a US Coast Guard veteran, my other brother and I put some oregano in a pipe, lit it, and passed it back and forth, in front of him. We were pretending it was pot. Big brother left the house mad as hell. He later called my mother and told her, that as long as my other brother and me were smoking marijuana at the house, he would no longer come over there.

Well, as I said, things are much better between us now. We will probably both have a good laugh, when he reads this – especially now that he has found a medical use for marijuana. Still, eight years or so, is a long time to wait for a joke to seem funny. Regaining a sense of caring for and from him, is the nicest thing that had happened to me in 1978. It must be a lot like thinking you have lost a loved one at sea, only to have them return to you, years later. So much to catch-up on, it is sad about the time lost. It would be much sadder, if no reunion ever took place. Makes me think about all those families, with divisions, that never do mend into understanding.

As during the past visit, with people from home, I won't be talking to you over the weekend. I do this with a purpose in mind. In order to make these tapes, as personal as I want them to be, I need to be alone in the cabin, while recording. Also, however, I do need the support that these visits from home give me. So, while guests are here, I will store up things to tell you. Talk to you on Monday. Have a nice weekend.

Richard Ebner

Monday, February 5
Almost breakfast time

Things have turned much colder, once again. I don't expect the temperature to rise above ten degrees today, and there is a strong wind blowing.

Tuesday, February 6
6:00 AM

More tree cutting needed. What, so soon?

Wednesday, February 7
Morning

Didn't cut a single tree yesterday. However, I did manage to get the truck stuck again. Thought I had better explain why, today will be tree cutting day, instead of yesterday. It took from about eight in the morning, until eight-thirty, last night, to get unstuck – with some breaks in between of course. Don't mean to exaggerate too much. I have been stuck more times, in the past three weeks, than during the past three years.

Thursday, February 8

I received a nice letter, from the owners of this camp, today, along with my first electric bill. The latter part of the letter, I could have done without – but, it was nice to hear from them, even if they were telling me that I owed them money.

Friday, February 9
Breakfast

Not a single grain of dog food, in Misty's dog-food barrel. This morning she will have to share my cereal and eggs. I don't think she will mind too much. It seems to be getting colder, each night this week. I caught something on the radio, about an artic high-pressure system coming this way, from out of Canada. I guess that means, it will be cold, and I should blame Canada.

Saturday, February 10
1:30 AM

So many times, in the past, I have sat in a chair, at this hour of the morning, with my headphones on and only a candle for light. I sat in a chair smoking pot and dreaming about being famous. From my chair, in my room, it was easy to be rich and famous. All I had to do was light up a joint, and I could be anyone. Sometimes, I would become famous by performing some amazing physical feat, like swimming the Atlantic Ocean. This particular fantasy was very strange for me, since my true swimming abilities barely take me the length of a swimming pool. And, I have a morbid fear of water from almost drowning when I was three.

With enough grass, I could imagine anything. I could be a famous basketball player, or a world-renowned lawyer. It didn't really matter much, who or what I was while stoned, as long as I wasn't me. Once I smoked myself into thinking I was the country's youngest president, winning by write-in votes.

My first job, as president, was to turn the White House into a museum and run the country out of an office building. This was not a fantasy that I had often. Not because it was any more implausible than any of the others – but, because it was not a job I would ever really want for myself.

One of my more popular, stoned-fantasies, was to be a rock star. Listening to the stereo, as I day-dreamed, helped make this fantasy seem real. I would pretend that I was performing the songs I was hearing, in an auditorium, live, somewhere. In the audience were all my friends and some of my enemies. Everyone loved me, of course!

Other times, I was a famous movie star. I would write, direct, and star, in my own films. When I won an academy award, I would turn it down. I would say, "It wasn't important to me." Hypocrisy existed even in my dreams.

When I was much younger, I remember being asked what kinds of things were important in life. Back then, I thought helping people was the most important thing you could do. What a good little kid, don't you think? As I got older, however, I began to wonder, if helping people ever would get me anywhere. Being very open and trusting as a young child, and being sensitive about other's needs, seemed to leave me hurting most of the time. Being rich and powerful started to take over, as being the most important things to obtain.

I soon learned, that unless you are born rich, being rich was not an easy thing to accomplish. Working hard, for something, was such an effort and the pay-off seemed so distant and unobtainable. I was just one person, in millions and millions, who were wishing they could be someone else, someone famous and rich, or at least, just rich.

When I discovered pot, I found a way to be rich and famous, without having to work at it. At night, alone in my chair, with my weed, I was rich and famous. When stoned, Theo felt much better, than the plain straight ambivalent Theo.

The idea of being famous still intrigues me, but for different reasons, from when I was stoned. Perhaps I have come full circle, back to the feelings of wanting to help people, like the way I felt as a young child. That is my desire – fame is not just for the recognition it would bring me, although that is still a part of it – but more importantly to me now, is the desire to be heard.

I feel that I now have some important things to say and famous people are listened to. Everyone wants to know what a famous person thinks and feels about life. Maybe, it is a need to have someone larger than yourself confirm some of the things you are thinking and feeling, as if it makes your own feeling more real and justifies your having them. Whatever the reason, being known to millions of people, gives what you have to say more weight.

If the idea of being famous intrigues me, it also scares me. It scares me, because of the lack of privacy that comes with being famous. As much as I want to tell the world about many of the things I am thinking and feeling, there is a part of me that I wish to keep private. It would seem that a writer has the best of both worlds. Not too many people would recognize most famous writers by sight – and yet, when they speak through their writing, millions hear them.

It is quite possibly premature to be sitting here, in this chair this morning, thinking about being famous again. On the other hand, I must be a lot closer to the possibility, while sitting here doing something about it, rather than, when I was sitting in a chair stoned, and just dreaming about it. And I am sure there are many others with important things to tell us, but various addictions have gotten in the way of their speaking up.

Sunday, February 11
10:00 PM

Cold, cold, cold – the radio is predicting it to be as cold as thirty-five below zero tonight, and I believe it! When I first thought of coming up here, to record this book, I figured that there would be so much free time, that I would have to invent things to do, in between taping. During this extreme cold, I have been so busy, just surviving, and trying to keep warm, that my problem has been trying to find the time to talk to you at all.

The temperature inside the cabin, right now, is fifty degrees. I haven't been able to raise it above that, since the sun went down. Before I go to bed, I hope to have it up to around sixty-five, in here. Even if I accomplish that, I know I will have to get up during the middle of the night to heat things up again. Since this is primarily, a summer cabin, the insulation leaves a lot to be desired. Sometimes it feels like I am trying to heat the whole out-doors, with two wood stoves. Imagine if I had done nothing to improve the insulation.

Richard Ebner

Monday, February 12
8:00 AM

It is so cold I don't want to get out of bed, at all today. Twelve blankets are piled on top of me now, and that makes it just warm enough to survive. The fires in the stoves have long since burned out. As of yet, I have not mustered up the courage to get out of bed and relight them.

Misty is curled up in the bed, with two of the twelve blankets, on top of her, with just her nose sticking out. The extra heat that her body provides, more than makes up for the lack of room, from letting her in the bed with me. Maybe, this is why dogs are considered man's best friend?

Monday
Noon

I couldn't stay in bed any later than eleven. By nine o'clock, I didn't want to sleep anymore – so, I tried to read in bed. By ten-thirty, my hands were frozen from turning the pages. This is already, the coldest winter I have ever spent, anywhere.

Monday
9:00 PM

Colder nights are yet to come. I find myself, laughing aloud, when I listen to predictions of fifty below zero, for tonight, in the higher elevations – not that I don't believe them. I think it's just a sign, that I am going crazy. After you have spent a few nights, at thirty below, what's the difference, between that, and fifty below? Twenty degrees, you say. Okay, smart ass, all I mean is that at a certain point colder loses its significance. Besides, my thermometer does not measure below minus twenty. During the day, it does not rise above zero. I don't know if that is an actual reading, or if the thermometer is frozen from the cold at night, and never gets a chance to thaw out, during the day.

Tuesday, February 13

I am sitting at the kitchen table, making bird feeders, out of plastic milk containers. It is very bright and sunny outside. Why, it even looks warm! Don't be fooled, it isn't. It still has not gotten above zero.

Richard Ebner

Wednesday, February 14

Don't you just love holidays like this? I do! Halloween and Valentine's Day are, perhaps, my two favorite holidays. Even though I am spending this one alone, I am not sad. I think it is better to be alone on Valentine's Day, knowing that someone loves you, than to be with someone, wondering if they do.

The arctic cold air mass is being very stubborn about leaving this area. Last night, and today, have been more of the same. Thirty to forty below, at night, and never getting above minus four, in the daytime. This cold could last straight through next week, according to the latest reports. Just think of all the lovely muscles I am building, from cutting and chopping, cutting, and chopping. Always try to look on the bright side of life!

Thursday, February 15
10:00 AM

I did a dumb, and then a stupid, thing today. Since the last time the bathroom pipes froze, I placed a small electric heater in the bathroom, to try to keep it from happening again. This morning, as I was taking a shower, I heard Misty barking at something outside. Not being able to tell what she was barking at, I turned off the shower and the heater to better listen. That was the dumb thing. The really stupid thing, was not turning the heater back on, when I left the bathroom. That's right, my bathroom pipes are frozen once again. I never did find out what was bothering Misty.

Friday, February 16
Sunset

I hate to keep talking about how cold it is here – but, that is at the center of my attention these days. The constant effort of providing enough wood, to keep the stoves burning, has drained my mental capacities, and left me with little time to think. When I do get a moment, to stop and talk into the recorder, like now, I find all that is on my mind is the cold.

I would like nothing better, than to be able to report a heatwave and get on with my stories of the past. Today, when I was out cutting trees, my eyelids froze shut – no kidding! Please cut me some slack, it has to get warmer sometime, I hope!

Saturday, February 17

I'm suffering from cabin fever, although, cabin chills would be a more appropriate name for the condition. It is just too cold to go out and enjoy the environment. Inside is too cold as well. Nothing can be done about it, except, to cut wood and wait for spring.

Sunday, February 18
Just before bed
The cold and the wind laugh at me – but, I am still here!

I get up and light the stoves, eat breakfast, cut and split wood. I feed the fire, feed myself lunch, and spit wood. Then I take Misty out for a short walk, a very short walk. Feed the fires, feed myself, and feed Misty.

Staying Stoned

I split more wood and put on more sweaters, as the sun goes down – I feed the fires. I pack the stoves full of wood for the night, and I know, they will only burn for a few hours, without more tending. I go to bed early, and try to fall asleep before it gets too cold. I wake up in the middle of the night, freezing, and relight the stoves. I try to think of something to say into the recorder, and give up after a few sentences. Then, I wonder aloud, why I am so tired, all the time. I go to bed and get up at the first light and ask the sun to stay a little longer today, while I cut more wood.

Another day is over and a new one has begun, with little hope, of it being any different. If only I wasn't all alone. If only, it wasn't all up to me! But, this is the way I planned it. I wanted this. It is mine! The cold and the wind are laughing at me. They work me like a slave, during the day. At night, the wind taunts me, whispering, "Give up, go home, to your warm bed. This is a hard life, and you like things easy," the wind chides me, as it blows through the cracks in my cabin walls. I go to bed wondering, "Is the wind is right?"

Monday, February 19
George Washington's birthday, and I am still here!

Richard Ebner

Tuesday, February 20
7:00 AM

The heatwave has hit. It is only seven o'clock, and already, the temperature is up to twenty degrees. After last week, I don't think, I will ever consider twenty degrees cold, anymore. I am going to light the stoves and make myself breakfast, now. Then I will get back to the recorder and stories of my seedy past.

9:30 AM
Smoking on the job, part three

Guru and I became friends, about a month after I started work, at P.B. Inc. Although we knew of each other, in high school, I never thought that we had anything in common, back then. From talking with Guru, since, I know he felt much the same way. That is why, when Guru started working at P.B. Inc., a month after I did, I never expected us to become friends.

Since both Guru and I were confirmed, on the job pot smokers, it did not take long, for each of us to recognize, that we did indeed have something in common. Somehow, when you are stoned, it is easy to tell when someone else is stoned also. Something in the eyes, and something about what one chooses to laugh at, gives it away.

Soon after Guru started work, we were smoking on the job together. When Guru was working the back elevator, we would ride the elevator to the fourth floor and stop it, between the fourth and fifth floors. There we would sit, smoke grass, and get to know each other. A bell inside the elevator would let us know, when someone needed it.

This system worked nicely and was a fool-proof way of smoking, on the job, without getting caught. Someone, on the bottom floors, needing the elevator, would look up the shaft, through the elevator door window, and see that the elevator was on the upper floor. They would just assume that Guru was doing his job, servicing someone on an upper floor.

If anyone rang for the elevator, on the fifth floor, Guru would take the elevator down to the fourth. Here he would let me off and let the smoke clear out, before returning to the fifth floor, to answer the bell.

I would go down the stairs and back to my truck, parked in an alley, between two of the buildings. The fourth and fifth floors, of the building that Guru's elevator serviced, were for warehouse space. Since most of the time, there was only one, warehouseman, for both floors, if someone rang for the elevator, on the fifth floor, it meant that no one was on the fourth and vice versa.

Other favorite places to smoke weed were – on the rooves of any of the buildings – my truck – the motor house, for the elevator, another place called "the hole" near the trash compactor – outside the Old Building – in our cars, in the parking lot, and, a favorite of mine – between rolls of fabric, on the fifth-floor warehouse. P.B. Inc., being located in a large, old mill complex, provided plenty of places to sneak a joint.

For the first year that Guru and I worked and smoked at P.B. Inc., the company was operating with two twelve-hour shifts, six days a week. This meant that I saw more of Guru, than he did of his wife. Judging by the way they got along, Guru preferred it that way. Out of those long work shifts, together, Guru and I developed a very close relationship, that extended to outside the workplace.

Of course, working from six at night, until six in the morning, six days a week, did not leave much time for a life outside of work. In the mornings though, after work, Guru and I would go to his apartment to smoke more grass, and talk about things that happened overnight. Much of the time, we'd complain about our large, fat, redneck boss, that both of us hated. Whenever there was no work on a Saturday, and sometimes, even when there was, Guru and I would go to a local bar, at six-thirty, in the morning.

Most often, the bar of our choice was Blackie's Bar. Well, it

Staying Stoned

wasn't really that we chose Blackie's but rather that Blackie chose us. That is, Blackie was willing to open its doors for P.B. Inc. workers at around seven, in the morning. This was an illegal procedure and someone said that Blackie had to pay the police off, with booze, in order to get away with it. I don't know if that was true, or not – but, during two years of drinking there, I never saw a cop.

I don't think that Blackie's would be anyone's bar of choice, actually. From the outside, the place looked as though, if you entered you would never come out again, alive. Had my car broken down, in front of Blackie's Bar, before I knew of the place, I wouldn't have gone in, even to make a phone call.

Conditions inside the bar were just as bad or worse. A couple of pin-ball machines, and one, very worn pool table, stood on a dirty wooden floor. Over the pool table was a single light, with a green metal shade. The bar, which ran along one wall, was unpadded. The stools were wooden, also unpadded, and many of them were broken. Behind the bar, was Blackie. A thin, old wiry man, who was quick to use his wooden stick, if a fight broke out, and many times, fights broke out.

For toilets, there were two wooden stalls, at the back of the building. From the smell, and the dampness, inside them, I think more people pissed on the floor, than in the toilets. There were no flashing lights, no pretty waitresses, and no loud music.

Blackie's was a poor working man's bar, with draft beer, for ten cents a glass. Never before had I been in any place like it. Without Guru, I wouldn't have had the nerve.

One of the things that impressed me, early on, in my friendship with Guru, was his ability to communicate with street people. He was very street-wise. I, on the other hand, was very street-wary. I wanted to learn how to become street-wise. I wanted to break out of my sheltered suburban life. Guru, seemed so comfortable talking to Blacks, Puerto Ricans, and other people. He knew the streets and knew what it meant to be tough, in order to survive. I was completely unlearned about this part of life. And, I knew that it showed.

As I said earlier, I did not think of myself as prejudice – at the time – but, I now know that I was. How could I not be, never having known anyone who was not white and middle class? At P.B. Inc., I had an instant education, in the many ways that a person could be prejudice. Some of my fellow workers, that were white, were openly prejudiced, and just plain hateful of anyone who was different. My boss took the prize, in this area. Others were prejudice, when it was convenient, and pretended not to be, when it was not.

Some of us, like me, were subtle in our prejudices. We laughed at the jokes told about Blacks, when they weren't around, hoping they didn't find out. When I was alone, with other Black workers, I felt uneasy, and I felt guilty. I felt guilty for laughing at the jokes and I felt guilty for being white, for being part of the race that stole these people from their homes, made slaves out of them, raped them, and continued to take advantage of them.

Through Guru, I was able to make friends, with some of the Black workers. At first, I just tagged along. Because Guru introduced me as his friend, the Blacks accepted me. I listened and learned.

One day, one of the Black workers invited me, to a place called the "Black Elks." It was a private club, in the basement of an old brick building, in Lowell. It was the Blackman's answer, to other clubs that did not allow Blacks to join. There was a pool-table and a couple of refrigerators filled with beer. We smoked some good reefer and I wound up confessing. It was the first time, I spoke honestly with a Black person, about my prejudices. To my surprise, they were very understanding. One Blackman told me, not to worry myself too much about it, because he was used to it. Becoming used to prejudice does not mean, that you accept it. It just means that you expect it.

One point made to me that night, really sticks with me, even now. There I was, the only white skinned person among about forty men with varying degrees of darker pigments, and I thought I was beginning to understand how they must feel to be outnumbered in society. When I expressed what I was thinking and feeling, I was told that no matter how hard I tried, I would never know how it feels to be Black, to be instantly recognized and identified, with white stereotypes of Blacks. It's something no white person can experience. I was told not to try so hard, and to just be myself.

It took some time for me, to gain the courage, to speak out against racial jokes. But from that night on, I no longer laughed at them.

Through our friendship, and our long talks, Guru provided me with a view of the world, that I knew I was missing, but did not know how to obtain. Knowing how to walk into a tough bar, in a strange part of the city, without getting punched out, is something they just don't teach, in school. You might ask, why do I think that is something a person needs to know?

It has long been my feeling, that the more each of us understands the similarities, as well as, the differences, in all people, the better the chances of improving life, for us all. Unknowingly, Guru taught me how to look for those similarities, in people. He taught me, to concentrate, on the things that are common, to all humans, and to realize that the differences are to be appreciated, and not feared.

For a relationship to be truly good, both parties must be willing and able, to offer something to each other. I have

Staying Stoned

already told you about some of the things, I think, Guru taught me. While I was learning, about people and life, from Guru, I think he was learning some things about himself, from me. All through high school and beyond, Guru had a low opinion of himself. Like me, Guru quit school and had to repeat a year, in order to finish, but for different reasons.

Guru's school experience left him feeling that he was dumb. On the other hand, I felt I was too smart, for school. I thought the teachers were the dumb ones – and, I set out to prove it, each year that I was in school. Even though I missed a lot of school, and when I was there, I was stoned a good deal of the time, I seemed to be able to get honor roll grades, whenever I wanted them. To me, this was an indication, that the school system was stupid and that I could get away with anything.

Recognizing that Guru was most certainly not stupid, I helped give him a renewed sense of confidence in himself. I kept telling him, that ignorance in certain things, was no measure of a person's intelligence. If he did poorly in school, it was most likely the school's fault. I gave Guru books to read, that supported the things I was telling him, and although, by his own admission, Guru was not much of a reader, he read them. Guru's opinion of himself started to change.

As life went on at P.B. Inc., Guru and I slipped into an almost unavoidable rut. Working nights, from six-to-six, we rarely saw the sun, especially, in the winter time. Our entire lives consisted of working, eating, sleeping, getting stoned, and getting drunk.

February 21
7:00 AM

What a heat wave. It made it all the way up to thirty-five degrees, yesterday. More snow is expected soon. Today, I will be doing some much needed cabin cleaning. Tomorrow, the plan is to climb Black Mountain.

Thursday, February 22
10:00 AM
A mountain, coydogs and deer

I have my camera over my shoulder, and my gun in the holster on my belt. I just need to get the snowshoes out of my truck, and then we will be ready to hike up the trail to Black Mountain.

Last night, while looking at the sky, Misty and I were witness to a fierce battle. Although we could not see anything. Around eleven o'clock, we heard the sounds of coydogs attacking something. Then there was an ire silence, followed by lots of howling. Misty was not impressed and told them so by barking. The whole valley echoed with the sounds, of coydogs and Misty. After the howling stopped, it sounded like the coydogs were fighting with each other. We could hear snarling and growling, followed by painful sounding, whimpering.

I suppose coydogs are related to coyotes. I don't even know if that is the correct name, for the animal. It is what the people up here call them, and that is good enough for me.

Oh, look at this, cute little rabbit footprints, in the snow. And look over here, bunny turds. Did you ever notice that rabbit shit looks a lot like rabbit food? You are what you eat, I guess. Never did find out if that rabbit hunter's Beagle returned.

Once again, I am being treated, to some of nature's most beautiful works. No, not the rabbit shit silly! The trees and the snow, the sounds of the birds, and a gentle breeze is blowing across my face. It is already a toasty, warm, thirty degrees, or at least it was, when I left the cabin. I wonder how ferns manage to stay so green, through the winter! I'm looking at Boston Ferns, I think.

"Ah, stay there, Misty." Misty wants her picture taken. Hold on, while I get the camera off my shoulder. Click, there, I got it.

She stopped to sniff something, in the woods, and wound up in front of a fallen pine tree. I just thought, the way she was standing, with the tree behind her, that it would make a nice photo. We shall see.

Incidentally, the camera I am using is a Yoshika thirty-five millimeter. I have three lenses for it, a wide angle, a telephoto, and a standard lens. There is also a way to delay the shutter so that I can take pictures of myself. Seems like a nice camera. I haven't had any pictures developed from it yet – and my only experience with photography is extremely limited – a Brownie camera is the most high-tech photographic equipment I have ever used in the past. There is an instruction book, but I haven't mastered it as of yet. I'll let you know how things turn out.

For those of you, who have never walked with snowshoes on, I am now going to tell you the trick to it. Make sure there is snow on the ground, before you start walking in them – and, always shuffle your feet with your toes pointed up. I know mother may have told you not to drag your feet, but it is necessary, when using snow shoes. If you don't, you will be doing more plowing and tripping than walking.

More footprints in the snow. I think we are on the track of those coydogs. The prints look a good deal smaller, than my Great Dane's, but there are many of them. They run across the trail, into the woods, and back across the trail again.

Looks like one of the dogs stopped to take a plop. Thanks to Misty, I didn't step in it. Sometimes, I think if there was only one dog turd, in the whole world, I would be the one to put my foot in it. It happens to me all the time, especially in the city. I wish people would learn how to curb their dogs. Oh well, it probably doesn't matter anyway. If they curbed their dog, I would step in it there, instead of, on the sidewalk.

We are about halfway up the trail, to the first meadow, on

Richard Ebner

Black Mountain. There are two meadows, on the way up the mountain. I am stopping here to rest for a moment. Misty is wondering what the hold-up is all about. Lots and lots of coydog tracks, right here. This must be an active spot for them. I hope they only like to eat, at night!

Moving on again, strange, I haven't seen any deer tracks. The coydogs around here must be hunting rabbit. Those are the only other tracks. Coydog tracks and coydog tracks, looks like they might have had a fight here. The snow is completely trampled and there are pieces of fur on the ground.

What's that? Oh my God, about ten feet off the trail, there is a deer! I should say, what's left of a deer. Its body is completely eaten away. The only fur left on it, is on the head – just totally mutilated. Its' entire backbone is exposed and there is no flesh at all. The legs are missing, even the bones are gone.

I promised we would see a deer. Never expected it to be like this! Well the coydogs weren't hunting rabbits. This must have been what Misty and I heard last night. They ate everything but the head, everything. Now, I am more and more glad I decided to take my brother up on is offer to loan me his gun. Nature can be just as cruel, as it is beautiful. I suppose I always knew that. However, having the once beautiful deer laid-out, in front of me this way, tends to drive the point home. I am going to take a picture, of the dead deer. I don't know if I will include it in this book or not. It depends on how I feel about it, later. God, what a mess!

As we continue up the trail, the coydog tracks are now bloody red. It looks as though each dog took a portion of the deer and dragged it to their own private picnic spot. Clumps of deer fur can be seen over here and over there. If they do this to cattle, I can understand why ranchers hate them and shoot them every chance they get.

The sight of the coydog's kill is behind me now. I am left with a feeling of shock – just not used to seeing a dead animal, in that way. The only animal flesh I have seen has been neatly cut and wrapped in the supermarket.

When I first thought of staying up here, by myself, it seemed like such a wild and courageous thing to do. Somehow, since viewing the aftermath of the coydog kill, my staying here in a cabin, with all the advantages of electricity and indoor plumbing, seems like a small achievement. As I sit, in my cabin, complaining about the cold, deer like the one I just saw, are outside in that cold. If I am hungry and there is no food in the house, I need only drive my nice heated truck, a few miles down to the general store. I don't have to stalk a deer, like the coydogs and kill it, with my bare teeth. There is no need for me to worry, that a strange noise, I hear at night, may be the last sound I ever hear, as the deer and rabbits must fear.

Humans, in this developed society, are such wimps. Not many of us would survive, without the trappings of our industrialized world. This is not a bad thing. I certainly don't want to trade places, with the coydog, or the deer – but, it does humble one, to think about what they must endure. Headed back to the safety of my cabin now.

5:00 PM

My present financial situation is like a small-scale version, of the national debt. This night will find me headed back to Massachusetts for a few days, to borrow some money, so this book recording project can continue. Talk to you when I return.

Monday, February 26
Back from Massachusetts

Massachusetts looked so strange, so grey – grey sky, grey trees, grey grass. Winter looks too depressing without the white stuff. Even though, seeing people at home felt good, I am glad to be back among the snow. I don't know how long the snow will last, even up here. The weather has turned very warm, now. It is all the way up to forty today.

Oh, and while I was down South, I had some of the photos

developed. Just to let you know, they came out okay, but I am not going to include the one of the torn apart deer. I had a hard time looking at it, and that picture is one I wish to forget. It is not the way I want to remember what a deer looks like.

2:00 PM

Since it is so toasty warm this afternoon, I thought we should take a walk down to the quarry and see if the ice has melted. If you've forgotten where the quarry is, just refer to your map. Here we are and water is once again flowing from the stream and into the quarry. Built in the late 1800's, it amazes me how well the stonework has help up. Those are all dry set stones – no mortar. Strange, since they had a kiln that they could have made mortar in. Perhaps the quarry was built before the kiln. Or maybe the kiln just produced lime.

Richard Ebner

The entire water supply for Lime Kiln Camps is gravity fed from the reservoir – no pumps needed. Any overflow finds its way down the stream, into the pond, over the dam, into the quarry and out into the stream again on the other side. Drinking water comes down from the reservoir through a series of pipes. Most of the time the pressure is sufficient for all the showers, sinks and toilets, even when the camp is full of guests. One exception to that can be the Hill House. That is where I stayed most often in the summer, and I can remember being all soaped up in the shower when suddenly the water would stop.

Oh, I realize I forgot to include this little foot bridge on the map. Not to worry, I'm sure there is still room to add it. Best be careful crossing over as there is still snow on it.

Safely across and headed back to the cabin now. All this talk about water and showers makes me realize I need one. Also, Misty's nails are getting a bit long and could use a trim. Talk again soon.

Wednesday, February 28
10:00 PM
My first cocaine and my first prostitute

Let me see, is this a leap year? No, I guess not, no one has proposed to me yet. That means this must be the last day, of this month. Two months gone already? My how time flies, when you are having fun. I just had to get that last line in somewhere.

At the beginning of my stay here, three months seemed like such a long time. Now, that I only have one month left, I don't know how I will find the time to tell you all the things, I still want say. Of course, since it has warmed up I won't need to spend as much time tending the fires.

When you hear the word 'prostitute', what kind of images come to mind – a tall woman wearing a low-cut dress and too much make-up? Perhaps, a woman wearing a blond wig and chewing bubble gum comes to mind, or maybe someone standing, on a street corner, in a short dress with black stockings? Those are pretty much the images conjured up in my head, before I met Diane.

I met Diane, while working at the second bus company, of my illustrious bus driving career. Diane and I started working there on the same day. She was also hired as a school bus driver. Are you surprised? I was not surprised that she drove a school bus, lots of women drive school busses. I was a little taken back, when, out of the blue, she told me, that, at night and on the weekends, she slept with men for money. To her, it was just a second job. Probably the fact, that she did not fit any of the stereotypes I had conjured up in my head about hookers, took me most by surprise.

Diane wore a leather motorcycle jacket and sneakers – as I did. I guessed her height to be about five-foot-eight or nine, with shoulder length black hair, sometimes loose and other times tied in a ponytail. She was pretty, but not stunningly beautiful. The only makeup I noticed was lipstick, and her eyelashes appeared to be natural. If she used perfume, it was subtle and I never noticed it. Her body was feminine, but not dainty or delicate. Diane had muscles and knew how to use them. This was not my typical image, of a helpless female, not by a long shot. During our company softball games, Diane was the secret weapon. She could swing a bat as well as any of the men.

One day, not long after she told me, about her second career,

Staying Stoned

Diane asked me if I had ever tried cocaine. Right from the first day at work, we were both aware, of a mutual interest, in drugs. Many afternoons, when our bus runs had been completed, Diane and I would smoke grass together and talk. I had never done any cocaine – and, that day, I told her so.

Next, she said she had some, and if I followed her home from work, she would turn me on. How could I, a lover of drugs, pass up an opportunity like that? I didn't pass it up.

At the time, Diane lived with two other women, also part-time prostitutes, in a house, in a nearby town. The women shared the rent and other household expenses. One of the women worked at a message parlor where they got many of their clients.

It was an unusually hot, early June, Friday afternoon, when I drove my beat-up, nineteen-sixty-six Jeep Wagoneer, in behind Diane's rather new looking Mustang. I remember thinking – 'She must be making more money than me.'

The house she was living in, looked like any other ordinary suburban house. There was a lawn that needed mowing. Since it was Friday, the Sunday afternoon ritual of pushing the lawnmower across the grass, had not taken place for almost a week. There were the standard row of bushes lining the front of the house. A fieldstone pathway marked the grooved route, to the front door. On the step outside the door, was your ordinary welcome-mat and token shoe scraper. From the outside, no one would suspect that three part-time prostitutes shared the space inside.

After being introduced to one of Diane's housemates, Diane and I sat down at the kitchen table. She asked if I wanted anything to drink. We took a quick inventory of the refrigerator's contents, and decided to share a Coke. How appropriate, don't you think?

Diane left the kitchen, to get her stash, leaving me there at the table tapping my fingers, and looking around the room. I don't know what I was expecting to find – flashing red lights on a pole, and posters announcing the girls' rates and services, maybe? When I looked out the back window, all I saw were a few flower beds, that needed watering, some lawn chairs, a dog on his dog-chain, and a clothesline.

Then I noticed it. All of the clothes, on the line, were women's clothes, bras and panties galore. That was not so unusual either. After all, three women lived there, and whether they were lawyers, bus drivers, or prostitutes, there wasn't anything really so strange, about all their clothes being women's clothes. I was not handling this situation too well. Why was I so nervous, about being in a house, where three prostitutes lived?

Before I had a chance to become too uptight, Diane returned

to the kitchen, with a mirror, a razorblade, and about a gram of cocaine, wrapped in a folded piece of paper. She placed the mirror on the table, and carefully unwrapped the paper over the mirror. Soon, she was busy using the razor blade to chop the lumpy white cocaine into a fine powder. Then, she separated the powder into small lines, each about one-inch long. Diane asked me for a dollar bill. She took the bill and rolled it tight, making a straw, to snort the cocaine.

"Do it up!" She said.

Guru had already taught me how to snort speed, with a dollar bill – so, I was pretty good at it. I think Diane was even impressed, with my technique. After I finished blasting one line, up each nostril, Diane snorted her lines. Then we sat around, and waited for the high to hit us. The burning sensation I felt, in my nose and throat, didn't really bother me. I was used to drugs that made you feel bad, before they made you feel good – comes with the territory.

Soon after we finished snorting, Diane said she was off. Judging by the look in her eyes, and the changes in her attitude, I would say she was off with a bang! She became very animated. A previous feeling of being tired, which she had expressed to me, was replaced, by energetic excitement. Her eyes became quite dilated, and her movements seemed to triple in speed. My eyes watched her, while my body remained still.

We continued sitting at the kitchen table, drinking our Cokes and talking about the different highs you get from various kinds of drugs. Diane asked me if I felt anything yet. I told her that my mouth and throat felt a little numb – but, besides that, I didn't really feel high. She told me that cocaine made her horny, and that she loved the buzz it gave her. I told her I loved to feel horny – but, the cocaine just wasn't doing it for me as of yet.

Diane complained about being hot and left the kitchen to put on some cooler clothing. She soon returned, wearing a bikini. Then she showed me a scar, on her leg, where her boyfriend had stabbed her. I was most interested to know, how she could still go out with him, after he did something like that to her. Diane said that most of the time, he was a nice guy. He just got mean, when he was drunk. I asked her if she was scared of him.

"Not really," she said. "I am used to fighting and having men try to beat me up."

As I sat there, talking to Diane, and looking at her sparsely covered body, I kept getting the feeling that she wanted me to do something – to take action. After all, I was a man, and men are supposed to act. What should I do, and what did she want? Was I supposed to grab her and rip her bikini off? Should I force her onto the kitchen table and take her right there, on top of the salt and pepper? Was she trying to interest me, in some professional sex, or was she just testing my reactions, with her free cocaine, her skimpy suit, and her sexual conversation?

Perhaps Diane was just being herself and I was reading more into her behavior than was there. Whatever the underlying messages, that were going on that afternoon between Diane and myself, it was clear to me, that I was not in control of the situation. If she wanted to have sex with me, for free or otherwise, I was unsure about it. If I wanted to have sex with Diane, I was unsure about that also.

My indecisiveness must have come across to Diane. One final time she checked back with me, to see if the cocaine had made me feel horny yet. My answer was still no. I asked her if she wanted to smoke some of the grass I had brought with me. At that remark, Diane seemed to get insulted.

"That was forty-dollars-worth, of good cocaine, you just snorted," she complained.

I told her I was sorry and offered to pay for what I had used. She refused my money, and left to go find her knife stabbing boyfriend. I went home. So much for my first cocaine experience.

Diane and I remained friends, and we continued to smoke pot together, after work. Never again though, did she turn me on to cocaine. Also, from that point on, I think she lost whatever sexual interest she might have had in me, if indeed she ever really did.

As with all drugs I have tried, my first experience with cocaine, was not my last. Sometime after that afternoon with Diane, Guru turned me on to a sample he had. Guru wanted me to help him buy some cocaine that we could resell, for a profit, and then be able to snort snow for free. I told him about my first experience with coke and how I never really got off to the stuff. Guru assured me, that he had some cocaine that was guaranteed to get me high. Once again, the offer for free drugs was too much for me to resist.

This time, the cocaine worked. I felt extremely euphoric. On top of the world, as they say. Oh shit, there is that dumb expression again. Anyway, I thought the high was great. Just when I was starting to get bored, with smoking grass, here was a drug that made me feel even better. One thing troubled me though, cocaine was so expensive. I was told not to worry. The larger the quantity we purchased, the lower the cost per gram. Since everyone loved to snort coke, Guru said we would have no trouble selling it. As Guru worked the figures out, on a piece of paper, I sat there enjoying my high.

We agreed to a plan, that had me putting up most of the capital and Guru doing all the selling. I was supposed to get my money back, from the first sales. Then, we would split the profits, fifty-fifty. High on cocaine, there seemed no way our plan could lose.

Staying Stoned

The next day, I used my credit card to get enough cash for Guru to make a quarter-ounce purchase of cocaine. We took the quarter-ounce back to Guru's place and weighed it out, separating it into one gram and half-gram amounts. Guru then folded little paper envelopes made from the pages of an adult magazine. We put the measured amounts into the envelopes and marked them.

Then we celebrated, by doing several lines of cocaine, that, according to his figures, would be paid for, once we sold the first packaged envelope. I again got a nice high, but noticed it never lasted very long. After about half an hour, I wanted to snort more. What the hell, it was free, right? Wrong!

Guru was a little concerned the police might be watching his house. I was a little concerned that Guru might snort up our whole purchase. It was decided that I should take most of the envelopes home, with me. When Guru had a buyer, I would just deliver what was needed. I put the envelopes of cocaine, in my underwear drawer, rolled up in a couple of pairs of socks, to store them until Guru called.

About two days later, I discovered that this was a bad idea. It had been very humid that week. Apparently, the cocaine absorbed the moisture in the air like a sponge. When I opened one of the envelopes, I discovered the white powder had turned to a clear mud like substance. I opened another one. It was the same. The entire purchase was unsellable. I was mad! But, what could I do? I hadn't purchased any moisture insurance, on our cocaine.

Back then, I think, financial and legal risks were the only things keeping me from becoming a full-time drug dealer. Morally, I didn't feel there was anything wrong in providing people with what they wanted. After all, if they didn't buy their drugs from me, there was always someone else willing to sell to them. The dealing I did do, was mostly to friends. I thought of myself, as a provider of good times, for my friends. They would get good pot, or other drugs, at a fair price, and I would make a small profit, that allowed me to get stoned for free. Being a chicken at heart, I never got into dealing on a large scale. The negative experience, with my first cocaine deal, contributed to my not expanding, as a drug dealer.

Even though cost was not a major reason, for wanting to stop doing drugs when I came up here, it is something I have given a lot of thought to since. Doing drugs for years, has cost me a lot of money. It has cost me the money I spent on the drugs, and it has cost me potential earnings. Earnings lost from all those days, when I just didn't feel like going to work and I stayed home to get stoned instead.

I guess I will never know, how much money doing drugs has cost me. When I was using them, it didn't seem to matter. I was spending my money on what I wanted to spend it on. Right now, I wish I had back even half of that money.

CHAPTER IV

March, 1979

Thursday, March 1

The weather is pretty much unchanged today. It's mild, in the low forties, and there is a slight breeze blowing.

Friday, March 2
3:30 PM
Another realization

While I decided to call this story *Staying Stoned*, I have come to the realization that most of my risky behavior actually occurred when I was drunk. With marijuana, I usually stayed in a relatively safe place and just enjoyed the buzz. Alcohol, on the other hand, had me looking for excitement and trouble.

Booze also made me feel invincible.

One night in particular comes to mind. Two of my high school buddies and I were driving around in my car while downing several beers each – a fairly common activity for us. This time we decided it would be cool to drive to Boston, about thirty-miles-away, and urinate on the Boston Commons' lawn.

Part of the challenge was to see if we could hold on long enough without peeing in our pants, or pulling over before reaching our destination goal. It was after eleven at night when we started down Route-3-South, towards Boston. Traffic was light and so far, everything was okay – aside from driving while intoxicated and underage. No problems either on Route-128. When we got to Route-2, my bladder started sending me signals, and my buddies said I'd better hurry up or they weren't going to make it.

I began to push the gas pedal down further and further, a little at a time. When we reached the section of highway where there is a long, and fairly steep decline, I could see the city lights on the other side of Mystic River below. We still had a few miles to go to reach Boston, and a few more to get to the Commons. I floored it! The highest number on the speedometer, of my seven-year-old, 1964, Ford *Galaxy* XL, V8 convertible, with bucket seats, topped out at 120-miles-per-hour. We buried it!

At the bottom of the hill I slowed down to negotiate the many intersections, traffic lights and rotaries ahead of us. Not seeing any other cars or cops, I blew through one of the red lights. Eventually, we made it to Storrow Drive, and ultimately to our finale destination. We all took a piss, and I drove us home.

The next morning, when I looked at my car's tires, I noticed that all four of them had the whitish looking cords showing. If any of those tires failed at the speeds we were going the night before, we'd have had more problems than just pissing in our pants.

Monday, March 5
10:00AM

It is raining today. I have opened all the doors and windows. I am enjoying the washing rain, that has freshened the stale air inside my cabin. Most of the snow is gone from my roof. It seems like only yesterday that I was contemplating having to shovel off the roof. I am not ready for spring. Already, I miss the snow, even though there is still much of it left on the ground.

My neighbors said that by leaving before April, I would miss the mud season. Right now, I am not so sure they were right. Two more weeks of winter would be perfect. I guess there is no point in wishing, when it comes to the weather. My faithful radio station is telling me that it will be warm, in the fifties, for at least a few more days. Did I complain when it was cold? I don't remember. No need for fifty below zero, but a little more snow would be nice.

Tuesday, March 6
8:30 AM

This morning there is not only rain, but pouring rain. No snow at all left on my roof. On the ground, there is still some snow, but only where it drifted, or where I plowed it into piles. I haven't been outside yet. It sure looks muddy out there. At least this weather should keep me inside working on this here book. I am only burning wood for a few hours each day now, and only in the small stove. The reduced effort of keeping this place warm, should also give me more time to talk to you. Now, if I can just think of something to say.

Escaping the farmhouse fire

Guru had already introduced me to speed before our cocaine disaster, so when he suggested we start selling crystal instead, I listened skeptically. A worker on the production line at P.B. Inc., would be our source. Apparently, this guy made the chalk, or speed, in his apartment, and he sold it in quantity for cheap. When Guru first introduced me to him on one of our breaks, he gave me the creeps. An extremely skinny man, and an extremely fast talker, who, when he wasn't talking, was grinding his teeth. I let Guru do the all the negotiating. And afterwards, I told Guru I didn't care if I ever met the guy again.

A few weeks later, on a Sunday, our only day off, Guru and I were in my car headed for Sanford, Maine. Guru learned of a party at a farmhouse, that several druggies he knew were renting for the winter. The owners were snow birds who went to Florida when things got too cold. This would be a great place to sell our newly purchased speed, Guru told me.

When we arrived, there were forty or more cars and several motorcycles parked on the snow-covered grass in front, and alongside the farmhouse. The bikers were the serious kind – no helmets. I usually stopped riding months earlier, but here it was January and these guys were still out there – a beer in everyone's hand. There were many more empties on the porch where they were gathered telling each other their stories. Clouds of cigarette smoke and swear words filled the air.

It was almost sunset, a little before 4:00 PM when we arrived. The smell of wood smoke was also in the air, but the top of the farmhouse chimney wasn't revealing much smoke – just some vapors that glistened in the low angles of the sun's light. I remember thinking that they must have a pretty hot fire going on inside.

Guru and I did another line of speed in my car, and finished our open bottles of beer before venturing inside. I was in no rush, and I felt very unsure about this whole adventure. Something was telling me to be cautious.

Once inside, Guru went looking for customers and his buddies that were hosting the event. As I had presumed, there was a raging fire in the fireplace – but I was surprised that there wasn't any screen in front of it. The entire downstairs was packed with people. More folks stood and sat on the stairway leading to the second floor. You could not move without being shoulder to shoulder with others. Most were smoking and drinking, so both hands were occupied. One needed to be careful not to bump into the hot end of a cigarette, or have a beer spilled on you.

The music was a loud mixture of Country and Rock, coming from speakers placed on top of stools in the corners of the living room. Those who were not moving to the beat, or singing along to the lyrics, seemed to be trying to have a conversation with one another. In groups of two or three, the conversationalists keep turning to each other, and alternating mouth to ear – ear to mouth.

In the dining room, it was a little quieter. There was a buffet of sorts – a couple of stacks of empty paper plates, more plates with small sub-rolls, filled with what looked like tuna in some, and egg salad in others, and several large bags of potato chips – no napkins. I wasn't hungry. Whenever I did speed, which wasn't very often and had only began recently, I didn't eat. Perhaps that is why Guru's supplier was so skinny?

This was bound to be a long night, and so far, I wasn't having any fun. After dark, the bikers came in. They quickly cleared themselves some space at the buffet table and began filling up. As one of them was about to sit down, he hesitated for a moment

Staying Stoned

to adjust something – that's when I noticed the pistol. More alarms started to go off in my head. As it turned out, the motorcyclists were not what I needed to worry about as they all left shortly after eating.

I wanted to go outside and take a walk, but I needed to remain where Guru could find me. Whenever he made a sale, I had to open my car for him so he could resupply. He didn't want to carry too many packets at one time.

After midnight, the party became unhinged. The firewood had run out, so people started breaking up the furniture and throwing chair legs and arm rests into the fireplace. Now I wished the armed bikers hadn't already left – they might have been willing and able to stop the mayhem. I needed to go. Guru and I connected up one more time, and I told him I wanted to out of there. He said he had one more sale to make, and then we could leave.

At 1:30 in the morning, Guru and I got back in my car and headed home. Two hours later I dropped him off at his apartment in North Chelmsford and went home to my place in Lowell. Later that day, I heard on the radio about a fire in Sanford, Maine, where a farmhouse had burnt down. The report mentioned that several Lowell residents were arrested on drug and arson charges. I began to worry that my name might come up during any investigations.

I called Guru, let him know about the fire, and told him I was done dealing. He agreed to buy me out, as I had furnished all the upfront money, and we split the profits from what he had already sold.

Escaping the farmhouse firehouse fire was an epiphany for me – it stopped my drug dealing ways. That was six-years-ago. My deciding to stop using, was more of a gradual awareness of questioning what I want to do with my life. I'm still asking myself that question, but I am asking it while sober. Whoops – got to go. "Misty, I hear you girl …"

11:30 AM
Close encounters with wildlife – too close

Sorry I had to leave so abruptly, but Misty was clearly in trouble and needed me. She was whimpering and scratching at the front door – two things she almost never does. When I opened the door, she had a whole new set of whiskers – porcupine quills.

Now if you are not as familiar with porcupines or their quills as I am, and this happened to your dog, you might have been panicking about getting her into the car and on the road to a veterinarian. However, I've been there before. Did you know, that when a porcupine is relaxed, you can pet them without getting your hands pricked? Always go in one direction – head to tail. Of course, it is hard to find relaxed porcupines in the wilderness, especially if a Great Dane is chasing them.

Anyway, I removed all the quills in Misty's face, one at a time, with many overly sweet-sounding expressions of, "Poor Misty," as I prepared her for the next yank. Contrary to some advice, I find it best to hold the embedded quill close to the contact point and pull straight out with a firm grip and a quick tug. Did you know that the quills of a porcupine have a natural antibiotic in them? This keeps them healthy when they accidently stick themselves – which happens. And fortunately for Misty, that antibiotic greatly lowers her chances of any infection.

Misty as financial sponsor of *Staying Stoned*

I realize I have been telling you mostly about the trouble Misty has gotten into while up here, and not so much about how helpful she has been. First of all, aside from helping to keep me

Staying Stoned

warm during some extremely cold nights, Misty actually financed most of this book/recording/writing experience.

When I bought Misty, from a supposedly reputable breeder last year, she was eleven months old and pregnant. None of we humans knew that she had puppies growing inside – but I feel sure that Misty knew. Within a few weeks it became obvious that she was pregnant. How many pups she would deliver and how many would survive remained a mystery.

On October eleventh, 1978, Misty gave birth to twelve puppies. The birthing process started at about eight in the morning and lasted through all of the daylight hours. Incidentally, that date is also my current girlfriend's birthdate. And, Girlfriend and I managed to be Misty's doula, without the need for a veterinarian. Once the puppies were born, and the cleanup was complete, we all rested.

In the weeks that followed, I began formulating a plan to make some money from the event to help finance my sabbatical up here. Two of the pups didn't look like they were doing so well – runt of the litter X2. I didn't think I could sell them, and I wasn't sure they were even going to survive. The other ten however, I knew could be worth some real money. The only problem was I didn't have any documentation on who the father was.

I contacted the breeder and offered them this deal – if they certified that one of the only two males that could have impregnated Misty was the father, I'd give them the pick of the litter. The breeder agreed and I let him decide who the dad was. That is how I got the paperwork I needed to sell the puppies as purebreds, and the breeder got a free male Harlequin Great Dane puppy. The suspected father was also a Harlequin – a big boy of about one-hundred-eighty pounds and thirty-three inches tall at the withers. And true to his namesake, he seemed like a bit if a clown when I met him.

Misty is a Merle, and when Harlequins and Merles mate you can get a variety of different colored pups, and some say, severe health issues – it is not recommended to breed them together. I don't think my breeders did that intentionally, as they didn't even know that Misty was in heat when the two dogs were shacked up together. Anyway, her brood consisted of: one Boston, seven Blacks, two Harlequins and two Merles like herself. Her lookalikes were the runts.

I kept making sure the little girls got their share of mother's milk by playing referee when the bigger ones wouldn't let them nurse. Both runts survived. One of them I gave away to a student studying to be a veterinarian. The other one I gave to the owner of this camp – who had recently lost her ten-year-old. After all, it was at this camp where I had been introduced to the breed in the first place, many years ago. The gift also secured my being allowed to stay here rent free. The remaining nine puppies I sold for a total of about three-thousand-dollars.

Friday, March 9
9:00 AM

This has been a winter of extremes – extreme cold, extreme icing, and now, extreme flooding. Reports from the radio tell me that the Connecticut River has overflowed its banks. People all along the New Hampshire and Vermont border have been flooded out. Fortunately, for me, I am on very high ground – without being high. The only problem I am experiencing is the mud messiness.

Sunday, March 11

It snowed, it snowed! Only about an inch or two, but it is much prettier than all that mud. Just enough snow to cover everything in white, once again.

Night of the Living Dead

After graduating high school, I worked in a popcorn factory for the summer, before I was scheduled to enter collage.

However, calling it a factory is a bit misleading. There were only four people working there – myself, my boss, the bookkeeper, and the owner. The building where we popped corn for the local drive-in's and the major movie theaters in downtown Boston, was a rundown, two bay warehouse in Lowell. Aside from the humans occupying the building five days a week during the day, at night, and on the weekends, the rodents owned the place – mice and rats.

My immediate boss, and coworker, Gary and I tended the popcorn kettle machine at the rear of the building, and received shipments of candy at the two loading docks in the front. Cases of various name-brand candies were stored on pallets directly on the floor. That was convenient for the nighttime occupants when they got the munchies. Part of our morning routine was checking the various traps, and separating out any of the candy boxes that had been broken into the night before. Oh, and one of my favorite jobs – sweeping up the rodent droppings.

The popcorn was cooked in an industrial sized kettle, using canola oil that came in five-gallon metal buckets. Tending the machine was tricky, and often messy. It was very easy to burn a batch if you didn't pay attention. And since Gary and I were quite often stoned at work, it was easy to lose track of time. The owner rarely came to the factory and he didn't seem to care that we smoked pot, as long as we didn't burn up too much of his profits. Betty, the bookkeeper, was only in the small office on Tuesdays. This left plenty of opportunities to get high.

After a batch was properly popped, we filled large, wax lined, paper bags with the product. Thursdays, Gary and I loaded a hundred or so of those bags, along with even more cases of candy, into an eighteen-foot box truck for delivery to the movie houses. Then it would be my job to drive the load into the city about thirty miles away. At the theaters, the staff there, discretely placed the already popped corn into the display popcorn machines and sold it as freshly popped corn. Yummy!

On my first trip to Boston, Gary was with me to show me the route. I remember him telling me, "If you get lost, whatever you do, never get onto Storrow Drive, or they will be pulling the truck, and you out from under an overpass!"

Gary was twenty-six and a Vietnam War veteran when I knew him. Twenty-six – as I am now, but with no desire to stop using drugs. He was originally from Schertz Texas, and he traveled back there from time to time to visit his parents. On his return, he would usually bring back some San Pedro cactus. That is how I was introduced to mescaline.

One Friday, near the end of our shift, Gary asked me if I'd like to try some, and then go see a movie with him while tripping. Since cactuses were organic, and people had been using mescaline for thousands of years, I wasn't afraid of it like

Richard Ebner

I was with LSD – never heard of anyone thinking they could fly on mescaline. Understanding what Gary wanted to use for the tripping part of things, I asked him what movie he wanted to see.

"Night of the Living Dead," he responded. "It is playing tonight at the drive-in on the boulevard."

Staying Stoned

I knew he was referring to the drive-in on Pawtucket Boulevard, which was also a customer of ours. But I had a hard time understanding why he wanted to see a horror movie – considering he had already told me how he suffered from shellshock after his army experiences in Vietnam. So, I asked him why horror? His response was that those movies allowed him to think of what happened to him in the jungle as fantasy. The more he watched horror movies, the less the memories of his own horrors seemed real. Who was I to judge what worked. Even though horror was not a genre, and still isn't, I had become Gary's friend, so I agreed to go.

The movie did nothing for me, but the cactus high was okay. Gary seemed to enjoy the film, as he laughed often. We left at close to eleven with Gary driving. On School Street, we encountered a taxi cab stopped in front of us. I heard the cab driver on his radio telling his dispatcher to send an ambulance. Gary and I got out of his car and walked up past the cab. There, in the middle of the road was the body and blood of a young man. At first, I wasn't sure if any of this was real, or if I was hallucinating. If I was hallucinating, so was Gary. A Lowell Gas Company tank was on my right, and in the road below is where the living night had ended for this twenty-something former life. Gary and I got back in his car, turned around, and drove home a different way before the police arrived.

Subsequently, Gary told me he heard that the formally living and now officially dead, young man, had been a student at Lowell Technological Institute. The story was that he had climbed up the gas tank and jumped off. Supposedly, he was hooked on heroine and failing in his studies when he committed suicide. I still don't know how much of these details were true, and if heroine was the reason for him thinking there was no way out of his predicament, or, if the expectations of academic achievement did him in. But, what a way to go!

I know my last comment might seem very cavalier, and in some ways, it is, but in other ways not so much. More sarcastic perhaps? If I indeed ever seriously consider killing myself, the last modus operandi I'd ever choose, would be jumping off something very high up. There are gentler ways to end one's life. However, I don't recommend any of them. Always wait one more day. Just saying. And just, perhaps, reach out for help. You never know, it might be worth staying alive, if not for yourself in that moment, then perhaps for someone else until you feel well enough to carry on.

After that experience, I never did mescaline again. Summer ended. I chose not to go to college, but instead got that job at P.B. Inc. that I already told you about. And Gary, the popcorn factory, and I, parted ways.

Monday, March 12
Why do people go to work?

It is tempting to think this last question is an easy one to answer, if not, a dumb one to ask. Ah, for money you well might say. So that we can buy food and clothing and shelter. A reasonable answer, as far as it goes. But It leaves a lot unexplained. When I had my first paycheck job in 1969, the minimum wage was $1.30 per hour. That is not enough money to provide anyone with a person's basic needs of food and shelter, let alone all the other expenses of living in a modern society.

In my past, I have driven all sorts of vehicles. Everything from school buses to lumber trucks. I have worked loading docks, from sunset to sunrise – and loaded trash compactors with nasty chemicals on them. Sometimes, my job was as a worker and sometimes, as a boss. I've pushed papers, in the clean coolness, of an air-conditioned office, and I've sweated in the hot sun, digging in the dirt. In a restaurant, I have washed dishes, served food, and smiled at even the rudest of customers.

During the middle of the night, while all the shoppers were sleeping, I scrapped the wax off supermarket floors. From nine-to-five, I have worked, and from three-to-eleven, and from six-to-six, and most other combinations of hours. Through it all, whether I was popping popcorn, at a popcorn factory, or selling rubbers at the local drug store, I have been wondering. Why do people go to work?

Those at the bottom of the economic ladder work because they have little choice. But what about the person who has already earned enough money to shelter, feed, and clothe themselves, for the rest of life, and yet, continues to work long hours each day. Does that person really work for money? I think not.

Maybe we work so that we can make the things that all people need, in order to live better lives. A noble try, at a noble answer, but I am afraid, it still leaves me wondering, if we really need all the things we think we do?

Before I start dumping on capitalism, let me first say I do not believe communism is a better answer. Although I do feel that certain needs, like healthcare, should not be 'for profit' businesses.

Furthermore, I am most appreciative of all the freedoms, our current form of government offers its people. Freedoms like being able to write this book and say anything choose to. But, something really troubles me about the capitalistic society in which we live. It seems to me, we live in a world were selling is of supreme importance. No longer does it matter if a given item is needed. Selling ability is the determining factor, as to whether something is produced, or whether it just dies, as an idea. Everything, from can-openers, to movies, and books, are produced, with one thought in mind. Will it sell? Will it make a profit?

Any capitalist reading this might ask, "Well, what is wrong with that? Isn't that the way things are supposed to be? It is the law of supply and demand!"

Unfortunately, when the law of supply and demand was establishing itself, as a sound concept in trade, no one could perceive how mass advertising, and particularly television, would distort the true nature of demand.

It used to be, if you needed a tool, to do a certain job and no one made such a tool, you would make it yourself. If you did not have the skills to make it, you would take it to your local blacksmith, who would make it for you. If the tool was good and useful, other people trying to do the same job would want one. This was good for the blacksmith, and possibly good for you, if the blacksmith shared with you some of what he earned from your idea. When enough people wanted your tool, and the blacksmith could no longer make them fast enough, a manufacturer would take over, all well and good.

A demand for an item was forcing the supply, of that item, to be increased. The manufacturers made a profit, which was good for them. Maybe it allowed for others to be hired to help make this needed tool, which was good for them. The people who needed the tool were able to get a useful item which made their own jobs easier. This was good for them. The law of supply and demand at work, with all parties concerned getting their needs met.

Today, the need for an item, and thus, the demand for that item, is not always determined by that item's usefulness. Through mass advertising, we are coerced and badgered and sometimes, even tricked, into thinking we need an item. Many times, we do not need it. Each year, millions of us buy things that we don't really need. Things that will clutter up our attics and lay around, in our garages, until we finally throw them away in disgust.

I can hear my capitalist friend saying: "Well, nobody forced them to buy anything."

And technically, that is correct. Nobody forced them to buy – but, the psychological pressures, placed on people through advertising, winds up being almost as strong of a force, to many people, as putting a gun to our heads and saying, "You must have this, buy it!" Most of us just can't resist items we are told will make us better looking, more desirable, easier to love, and happier.

If advertisers thought they could get away with it, they

would package a box of air, calling it, *Happiness in a Box*, and sell it by the millions. In a large way, this is just what they are doing, by conning us into thinking material things can be a true source of happiness. When demand starts being determined by an advertiser's imagination, and by big business's need to show a quick profit, for its stockholders, then items that are truly needed may be over-looked, because they are not as sellable.

Some ideas for products, that might be better than the products currently available, are held up in the idea stage, because, if developed, they would interfere with the sales ability of the current product. Oil companies are not going to be too quick about finding and developing alternative forms of energy, as long as they have oil to sell.

Other good ideas, that may be needed, where there is a clear demand from the public, never get off the drawing board, because people in control of the money, and thus advertising dollars, that it takes to make something profitable, aren't willing to risk that money. A good example of this is in books. Someone who is well known, which you can equate with being well advertised, will have little trouble finding a publisher for their book. It won't even matter much, what the book is about, or how many other books have been written on the same subject.

The well-known person's book is sellable, because she or he is sellable. An unknown author, on the other hand, is a big risk, for a publisher. Even if the book is well written and addresses a subject that needs addressing, few publishers will be willing to commit advertising money, to that book, much less publish it. That is why I will be lucky, if you ever do get to read this.

The quality of a product is something that also suffers, when profit and sales are the most important things, to a company. As most of the family run businesses get bought up by large corporations, there is no longer the concern, that the products produced by those companies reflect someone's personal integrity.

No one can be held accountable for the quality of a product anymore. If a product falls apart in two years, when it should have lasted five, it just means that another one can be sold three years early. That kind of thinking is good for profits but bad for the consumer. It used to be that if you did not like the way a certain product held up, you wouldn't buy from that company again. Today it is hard to know what company is really behind the making of the item you purchase. Some companies produce items that are basically the same, under different names. Big conglomerates have all but taken the competition out of capitalism, in this country. This has been especially true, in the pharmaceutical industry.

Even when a product lasts a reasonable amount of time, advertisers and profit-hungry manufacturers are busy finding ways to make us think we need a new one, before the one we have has really outlived its usefulness.

In my carpentry business, I have had requests from customers to build them a new kitchen, when the one they had was only seven-years-old, and fully functional. The seven-year itch? For some, remodeling has become a fashion statement.

What does this all have to do with my original question of why do people go to work? Furthermore, what does any of this have to do with a book about drugs. A friend of mine once said that the only reason we don't have solar energy yet is because no one has found a way to put a meter on the sun. This kind of cynical remark reflects an attitude, in this country, that nothing is important unless there is a financial profit to be made. It also reflects a feeling that is shared by me, and I think, shared by much of today's youth – we will never be able to afford all those things the advertisers keep telling us that we need in order to be happy.

Every day we are told, on the news, that fewer and fewer people will be able to afford a house. How can a person fulfill the American Dream, if they can't even afford to buy a home, no matter how hard they work and how much they try to save? It leaves a person wondering – why do people work?

For the youth that gives up that childhood dream of becoming a doctor, or a lawyer, or the president of some large company, which by the way is most of us, the reality of never being able to afford the things the adult world has been telling us are necessary in order to be important people, makes the future seem futile.

It also makes drugs look very attractive. At least when you are high, you can feel good and you can feel important. Best of all, with drugs, you don't have to wait. Everyone can afford a joint here, or a hit of speed there. For me, drugs even allowed me to forget reality for a while and start dreaming, once again, that someday I would be able to afford all those things advertisers say I need in order to feel happy. When I came down however, I was still left wondering, why do I work at all, which many times left me so depressed, I would get high again, and not go to work.

I realize that none of what I have said explains why so many rich people use drugs. Not being one of them, I'm not sure I know why. I do have my guesses though. Rich people are just as caught up in the capitalistic material trap, as are poor people. They can afford to buy all those things, advertisers tell all of us we need in order to be important, happy people – but, once they buy them, they discover they really aren't any happier. What a shattering discovery that must be.

It is beginning to sound like a catch-22. The poor can't be happy because they can't afford to buy the things that will make them happy, so they drink and take drugs. The rich drink and take drugs because their material possessions do not give them lasting happiness. No one is really happy. We are all just high on delusion.

So, what is the answer to finding happiness? What will stop people like me from wondering, "Why go to work?" I am not at all sure I have figured that out yet, but I do have some ideas. As a society, we need to place more importance on the value of the individual, both in an out of the work place. Besides being paid a wage that can actually sustain them, a worker must know that she or he is not just one more expendable part of a huge conglomerate.

Workers need to feel they have a stake in the work that they trade so much of their life's time, in order to perform. Profit sharing and management-labor-idea-sharing are two important steps in that direction. More is needed.

Outside the work place, we must become more aware of the things that separate humans from animals. This is language and the ability to create. Supporting the arts is so very important. Art may be the only reason for humans to exist. Ever see a cat paint a picture, or a dog write a play? Sorry Misty – you are still very much loved and valuable to me.

Being involved in the arts, whether as a spectator, or as a participant, is one of the ways you can really bring some happiness into your life. Spending money seeing a play, which you will have in your memory for a longtime, is a lot better than buying that useless item that will sit in your attic, until you throw it way. Somehow, I feel sure, it is not man's purpose in life, to turn all iron ore into automobiles, and all fossil fuels into useless plastic junk. I hope, at least, that is not why we are all here.

Since we are all consumers, perhaps we can force manufacturers to produce items that are truly needed. Once we realize, advertisers are willing to tell us anything, they think we want to hear in order to sell us, and once we realize, advertisers don't really give a shit, if whether what they sell us is what we need, then maybe we can change their tune. Remember, if we don't buy what they are selling, then the companies they represent won't make a profit. If companies don't make a profit on what they would like to sell us, they might begin to ask us what we need. Perhaps?

It is time to remove some of the emphasis on profits. Sure, a company needs to make a profit – but, it is time to give some of that profit back to the poor people, who buy: food, shelter, soap, cars, televisions, antacid tablets, hair care products, and the insulin they can't live without. I mean, profit, sure, by all means please do make a profit. But, when is enough, enough?

No, I do not wish to dictate how much is enough. I don't

even resent the rich being rich. I realize they may be much smarter than us poorer people – and, they may have worked very hard, to get rich. I think some may even deserve to be rich. I don't want to take that away from anyone – but, when will the wealthy be satisfied? How many cars, and boats, and planes, and houses, does one person or their family really need?

What I am looking for is the return of the philanthropist. A return of those people, whom, after having secured their own financial independence, donate themselves and some of their resources, to making this a better world, for all of us. I know that many wealthy people donate large sums of money to charities. This is good, and I praise them for that.

However, my definition of a philanthropist goes beyond just passive contribution. I think of a philanthropist, as someone who is an active, participating facilitator, as well as a donator of funds. This is a person, who not only gives money to a charity, but who gives of themselves, as well. Someone, who is a teacher about life, and an example, for the reasons of supporting a quality human existence for all, that for me, is a philanthropist. And that could be a good person to work for if it is not possible to become one yourself.

In 1978, when I took a break from 'working', in the traditional sense of what that means, the minimum wage had climbed to a whopping $2.65 – still not enough for one person to survive on, without working many more than forty-hours per week.

However, even though, at my own expense, I have actually worked harder up here in the mountains than at any of the jobs that I was previously paid for, I feel I have gained more than I have lost. Finally, I have found a fulfilling reason to go to work.

Wednesday, March 14
"Are you scared of me Kid?"

One cold night early in my career as a truck driver for P.B. Inc., I was assigned to the Old Building. It was a one employee operation over there, and the regular guy had called in sick at the last minute. Since my driver services were not needed that night, I was the most logical choice to fill in.

The Old Building consisted of; a receiving dock, warehouse space, a small office with a space heater, a desk, a phone and a filling cabinet. The tasks included; unloading delivery trucks of large rolls of fabric with a forklift, paperwork, and keeping things neat and tidy. It was a lonely job and often quite boring.

On this particular night, all my work was done by eleven pm. Seven more hours until quitting time. I decided to smoke a joint and eat my supper – two peanut butter sandwiches and a bag of chips.

I opened the door next to the loading dock so that the marijuana smells could dissipate into the night air and not stink up the joint. That is when I noticed a large man riffling through the trash dumpster. Hesitantly, I called out to him, "Can I help you?" I asked.

"Got anything to eat?" he replied.

This guy looked cold and hungry. I felt empathetic to his condition. However, he was also at least three-inches taller than me, and probably a hundred pounds heavier. Also, technically he was trespassing. What to do?

I invited him in and shared my food with him. We talked for time. Mostly, he asked me about my job. I answered politely, and didn't question him about anything. Pot smoking never came up, but I felt sure he smelled it.

Around midnight, the phone rang. It was my boss calling over from the main building. "The police are here looking for a large black man. Have you seen anybody over there?" he asked.

"Yes."

"A tall heavyset black guy?"

"Yes."

"Is he still there?"

"Yes."

"Good! He is wanted in connection with a recent murder. Keep him there. The police will be right over."

I hung up without saying anything further. But inside my head I questioned my instructions, and decided I was definitely not going to, 'Keep him.' If this tall heavyset Blackman chose to leave, that would be his choice.

Perhaps sensing my nervousness, my newly found dinner guest asked, "Are you scared of me Kid?"

I, in turn, asked him, "Should I be?"

He started to laugh, and then said, "Hell no! You just shared your meal with me. I never bite the hand that feeds me."

Soon after that, three police cars pulled up in front of the loading dock – no sirens blaring – no flashing lights. Six cops entered the building and one immediately started shouting instruction, "Get up slowly! Put your hands behind your back!" The commanding officer pointed. "Now walk over and face that wall!" Two of the other cops frisked him and put on his handcuffs.

As they led him out of the building, he looked over his shoulder at me, and thanked me. There was no sarcastic tone in his voice – only a warm smile on his face.

Now Time

So, it is still Wednesday, March 14,1979 – in now time for me, despite when you are actually reading this. I realize that the telling of my past, comes to you in no particular sequential order. My apologizes if this is off putting for you. It is not done to deliberately confuse or disorientate. When I remember something, or think of something I want to talk about, it just comes out. May you be grounded by the "real-time" dates I give you.

I would like to go back to P.B. Inc. now, and briefly tell you about my last eight months working there. Eight months before I was laid off, I was made the youngest working foreman, in the company's history. They put me in charge of all shipping, receiving, and warehousing, for the company's second shift, three-to-eleven, operations. During the summer, before my promotion, I stopped my use of drugs on the job and began to prove myself, as a leader. My efforts paid off very quickly. I was promoted to acting foreman. Then, three months later, I was promoted to foreman.

At first, my promotion was the best high of my life. Finally, I was being given the opportunity to use my skills of relating to people, in a meaningful way. Now, I would be able to put my idea of humane management into force. I could correct all the things I had felt were wrong, with the way my boss had treated his workers. So, I thought!

In the beginning, things went very well for me. I was high on myself, all the time, and I think that feeling transmitted to my workers. One of my best successes was establishing a good working relationship with a man called, Cappy. He was in charge of the shipping department, on the second shift, at the time of my promotion to foreman. In his fifties and having worked for the company over many years, Cappy felt sure that he would be promoted to foreman, of the entire department, when the job opened up. A robust little man, with a booming voice, and a very loud laugh.

It must have been devastating for him, to be passed over, for the job. Even more devastating must have been the fact, the one they chose, was only nineteen and had only worked at P.B. Inc., for a little over a year. When I took over as foreman, I was very much aware of Cappy's resentment toward me. Through time and understanding, however, I was able to change his attitude. We became good friends, who worked well together.

Although I was technically his boss, I tried to never use my position in an authoritarian way. To me, we were just two equally important people with a common job to do. I always tried to recognize and support Cappy's knowledge of his job, which, in the shipping department, was much greater than my own. He became one of my strongest allies, at work. Together, we made the second shift shipping department, the most productive, in the company.

I tried to use that same kind of support and understanding

with the rest of my workers. It paid off. Before long, the second shift was leading the other two shifts, in many important areas. We started to have the lowest absenteeism and best safety record. Our shift began to be held-up, as the model, for the other shifts. In general, we operated more efficiently.

Then things started to change. Upper management was trying to stop a union from forming in the company. Instead of listening to the workers complaints, the big bosses got paranoid and became very suspicious, of all their workers. They began establishing more rules to keep tighter control, and they started enforcing many rules that used to be overlooked. Word came down, from up top, for all foremen to be stricter with their workers. We were ordered to start files on our workers, and to write down, in those files, anytime one of them broke any of the rules.

Since all the big bosses went home, at five o'clock, most of my shift was free from their interference and control. When the clampdown campaign first started, I was able to shield my workers from it. I did things the company's way, until five, and after five, I ran things my way. This worked for a while. My workers continued to go all out for me and I continued to treat them as people. I would bend the rules, when the rules seemed less important than the overall output, of the work getting done. If a worker took twenty minutes for a coffee break, instead of fifteen, as company rules stated, I didn't care. I knew that same worker would work right through his coffee break, when I needed it. My workers respected me and I respected them. We worked as a team and things continued to go well.

Then, the big bosses started to come in at night, unannounced, and check up on things. They found my workers, on coffee breaks, during non-designated times – shame on them! I was placed on report to my boss. He, in turn, put pressure on me to follow the rules. I tried, in vain, to point out that the second shift worked better overall, then the other shifts. The record showed things worked more efficiently, my way. My boss even acknowledged this. I was still told to do things by the book.

This was something I had a very hard time understanding. My relationship with my workers felt more important than following my bosses' orders. I continued to bend the rules.

One of my best workers had a family responsibility that conflicted with his getting to work on time for his three-o'clock shift. He needed to pick up his daughter from school. This made him fifteen minutes late to punch in. So, I signed his card for him each day. Then he would punch out on time, but stay working for me the additional fifteen minutes past the official end of his shift – sometimes even longer. This exception to the rules cost the company nothing, and in fact helped them maintain an exceptional employee that never missed a day of work.

Eventually we both got caught. I was told to fire my best worker for being late, even though he always made up the time at the end of his shift. When my job was put on the line, I gave in. I enforced the rules but no longer cared about doing the extra things, which made the second shift more productive.

I controlled the length of my workers coffee breaks. Gone were my attempts at inspiring them to treat work as a challenge, and to do it better than anyone else. When I gave in, my workers gave up. They followed the rules but would give nothing extra of themselves. The team spirit died. I became less and less interested, with going to work. The high for me was gone.

I started to take days off. When I did go to work, I started to do drugs once again. Sometimes, I would have to take a hit of speed, just to get up the motivation.

A few months after, a union was voted in, by the workers, at P.B. Inc. I was laid off. It was nothing personal, they said. It was just that in order to pay the union wages, and because of a slowdown in sales, they had to let some people go. The ironic thing is that before the crack-down by the big bosses, my workers had all told me they did not want a union.

So, that was the end my career, as the youngest foreman ever to work for P.B. Inc. I was not the only one to be laid off, just the first. That summer, I heard from some of my former workers that, my boss and my former boss, were also let go.

Before winter came that year, many of the big bosses also found themselves, out of work. To my great delight, I learned that the one who came in to spy on me, and my workers, was eventually fired. Hundreds of workers also lost their jobs, in a big company shake-up. It is sad, and the saddest thing is, it didn't have to be that way.

Thursday, March 15
11:30PM

During the next few days, I will be preparing to leave this cabin and go back to the real world. On the twenty-fifth, of this month, I will have completed the contract I made with myself, to spend three months in these mountains, without using any drugs.

Although I would like to stay, my lack of money, will not permit this. I hope the stories of my frustrations, in my various jobs, did not bum you out too much. That was certainly not my purpose in telling you them. It is my hope you will be able to use these stories, to make you own work situations better, and more satisfying ones, good night.

Saturday, March 17
10:30 PM
DWI and stopped with guns drawn

Sometimes my memory of dates becomes blurred over time, but I believe it was in the summer of 1973, that a neighborhood friend of mine, and his sister, traveled with me to Tanglewood, in Lenox, Mass., to witness a concert with John Denver.

From Chelmsford, Mass to Lenox is about a two-and-a-half-hour trip. Before we left, there was much to do. Aside from finding a couple of beach-blankets to bring with us, there were libations to prepare.

If you have never been to Tanglewood, and even if you have, there are two choices for seating – inside the Koussevitzky Music Shed, or on the lawn. The three of us were definitely lawn kind of people. If we had all been of legal drinking age, we could have bought beer at the show and drank it in the designated drinking area. No alcohol was allowed inside the shed. On the lawn, coolers and booze were okay as long as you were old enough – but not all of us were. Brother and sister were seventeen and sixteen, and had we tried to drink openly, security might have caught them, and I could have been arrested for providing liquor to minors.

Which brings us back to preparing the libations. Aside from rolling several joints, that we intended to smoke in my car before entering the grounds, we wanted something to drink during the show. A previous experience of smuggling booze into a baseball game at Fenway Park had proved very successful, so I just repeated the process.

The day before the concert I bought a six-pack of Orange Crush in glass bottles with metal caps, and two-fifths of vodka. My cohort from our old baseball smuggling days, loaned me his bottle capping tool. This device allowed you to re-squeeze metal caps, one at a time, onto bottles, that when done properly, looked like they had come directly from the manufacturer without ever being opened. The tool itself looked like a small grapefruit press.

During the initial process of removing the caps, it was important not to dent them, or scratch the paint. So, we placed masking tape on top, and then using a bottle cap opener, we slowly pulled up at multiple locations, circling around and around until the caps were freed from the bottles.

Next, we poured off approximately half of the soda, and replaced it with the vodka. These were twelve-ounce bottles, so we now had six ounces of liquor in every one – some pretty strong, Orange-Crush-Screwdrivers.

Then, before getting into my car, we each had one for the

road. A bad expression, and a bad idea. Once there, we parked far away from the event, smoked a few joints, and drank more of our homemade screwdrivers.

I don't actually remember much of the concert and we left before it was over. My stronger memories come later, and will be revealed soon. So, as we walked back to where I had parked, it was definitely an effort. You might say we were running on empty. Once there, brother and sister climbed into the back seat and promptly passed out. I covered them with our beach-blankets, and got myself into the driver's seat.

There was one screwdriver left that I chose not to drink. Placing it on the passenger seat, I then started the car. Before putting it in drive, I gave myself a pep talk. "Just stay within the speed limit and you will be fine." I rolled the windows down before heading off, thinking the rushing air would help keep me alert and awake.

And I was fine, for the first hour-and-a-half or so. Just after Worchester I noticed a State Police cruiser parked in the breakdown lane of Route 290 with its lights off. As I passed by the cruiser, it pulled onto the highway and quickly caught up behind me. Even though I wasn't exceeding the speed limit, instinctively I backed off the gas petal. That is when things began being, not so fine.

My four-year-old, little two door Maverick was in need of a

tune up and a muffler. The sudden reduction in fuel caused the engine to backfire several times. Then my rearview mirror was lit up with blue lights.

I put my right directional on and maneuvered over to the breakdown lane. Since my windows were already rolled down, I just kept both hands on the steering wheel in plain sight as the two officers approached. Looking in the side mirrors, I noticed that each of them had their guns drawn – not pointed at me, but at the ready by their sides.

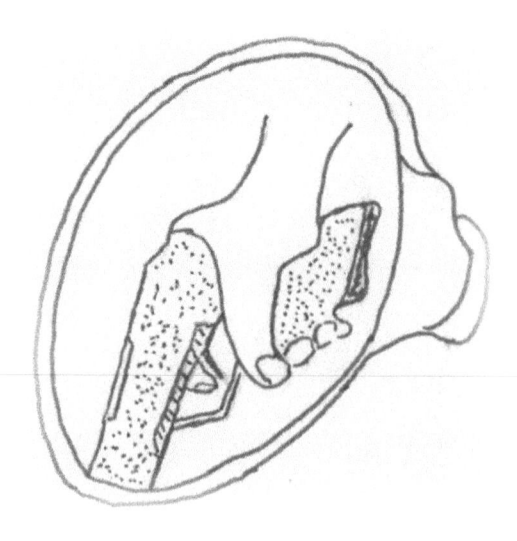

The cop on my side, shined his flashlight at my face, and then he slowly holstered his pistol. On the passenger side, the other one directed his light into the backseat, where my coconspirators were still asleep. Then he put his gun away as well.

"License and registration," the officer on my side commanded.

Before moving a muscle, I told him where the documents were, and waited for him to acknowledge that it was okay for me to open the glove compartment, and to reach into my back pocket for my wallet. Both flashlights remained trained on me and all my movements during the entire process.

The two officers took my documents and moved to the back of my car for a powwow. One cop grabbed everything and went back to the cruiser – presumably to call it in. The other one came back to my window.

"What's with your buddies in back? They been drinking?" he asked.

"Oh no! They are Catholics, and their parents would kill them if they drank. They are brother and sister by the way." That was my quick response, but I knew I'd need to come up with something more, if I was to get away with this without being arrested. And I felt sure that telling a State Cop, that we had all just been to a rock concert, wouldn't help my cause. So, I made up a story.

"Where you coming from?" was the officer's next question.

Oh, we were hiking and climbing in the Catskills – Upstate

New York – you know?"

"I know where the mountains are," he responded in a rather pissed-off tone.

"I'm sorry, of course you would. Well, anyway, the brother and sister team in my back seat are complete newbies' to hiking and climbing. I think I pushed them too far, too fast."

Just then, the second cop came back and said all my stuff checked out okay – no outstanding warrants – not even an unpaid parking ticket.

"Okay young man, you're free to go," cop one said.

"Can I ask you a question?"

"Go ahead."

"I couldn't help but notice that when you first came up to my car you both had your guns out. Is that normal for a traffic stop?" I asked.

"This wasn't a normal traffic stop. We were looking for a car involved in an armed robbery earlier tonight. Your car fit the description. And, when it back-fired we thought we were being shot at. Which reminds me – you need to get your muffler replaced!"

"Oh, I'm so sorry! Actually, I have an appointment to replace it next week," I told him.

"Well make sure you do it! Have a good night and get home safely."

Staying Stoned

That was it. I couldn't believe my luck. They got back in their cruiser and left. I didn't even have to get out of my car. No sobriety test – no questions about the bottle of Crush on the passenger seat next to me – no searching my trunk to look for the grass, hidden in a box of road flares – not even a written warning about the muffler.

So, why was I so lucky, if lucky is what you'd call it? I was fortunate that I didn't crash the car, injuring or maybe killing us. But other than that, perhaps I was unlucky? If I had been forced to walk the line, and I couldn't, what then? Perhaps I would have learned earlier, what I now know – eventually your luck will run out if you drive under the influence of substances other than your own internal hormones – and even those, can be dangerous.

However, I do still speculate as to why I was treated so gently by those two officers. Was it because we were young white kids, and they were both white cops of an age where they could have had their own teenage sons and/or daughters? Who knows for certain?

And just another few words in support of what cops' jobs require. Can you imagine what it is like pulling up behind a car at night, never knowing what the intent is of the driver you've just stopped? Or being called to stop a fight between a husband and wife, only to have them both turn on you?

Most of my interactions with the police have been positive ones. Growing up in a house with repeated domestic violence, the cops that were often called by our neighbors when things got too loud, truly were, peacekeepers. They were the only ones who could stop the insanity, even if, only until the next time things got crazy.

As a teenager hanging out with my friends in our neighborhood, my buddies would hide when we saw a cop car coming up the street. It didn't matter that most of the time we weren't doing anything illegal – it's just what you did. Except me. I waited, smiled and waved as the cops passed by. I knew many of them by sight if not also by name. Sometimes they'd stop, roll the window down and ask me how I was doing.

Thursday, March 22
4:00 PM

Just now, as I was walking back from returning those snowshoes I had borrowed, there was the makings of a terrific photograph. With the sun still out, I noticed you could also see the moon, high in the sky, hovering over Black Mountain. Overnight snow left some of the white stuff on the branches of the trees. By lining my camera up, with one of the branches and the moon in the sky, in a certain way, it looked like the moon was sitting on the snow-covered branch. Added to this was an eerie effect, in the color of Black Mountain, caused by the sun, at my back, shinning at a low angle through the trees. I clicked off a couple of pictures. I hope one comes out? If so, it might make a good cover for the book.

Sunday, March 25
Packing up to go home

Let me see, what's left to be done around here? I need to pack up my: stereo receiver, turntable, one-hundred or so vinyl record albums, Roget's International Thesaurus, American Heritage Dictionary, 1957 twenty-six-volume World Book Encyclopedia, and clothing. Better check under the bed. Mother always told me to look under the bed, before you leave someplace that you will not be going back to for a while. You see that? Mother was right, I found a pair of socks and one of Misty's chew bones.

Here I am loading my plow into the back of my truck. Man, that thing is heavy!

Now for some meditation and self-reflection before I leave this beautiful and inspiring wilderness. I think I will try and make meditation my new way of getting high!

I am stalling around, because I just don't know how to say good-bye. Over the course of the last three months, I have come to enjoy my life of semi-isolation. The depression of the first few days seems so distant now. I have grown accustomed to my life of cutting wood, taking long walks with Misty in the snow, at night. I have grown accustomed to talking to you. I like my life, here in the mountains. I don't want to leave.

Be that as it may, I am packing up to go home now, and I feel I must try to put what I have done here into some sort of perspective. I have shared, with you, many personal things about my past. This was not done because I think I have led such an inspiring life. My purpose in being open and honest with you, about my feelings, both past and present, is to help you become more honest and open about yourself. It seems to me, self-examination is really the only way we can force growth and change to occur in our lives. A life without growth, isn't worth the effort of staying alive.

I feel I have done a lot of growing, these past few months. This experience has been good for me, so it pleases me, where I have come to in my life – and, it concerns me, where I am headed. I am proud of not doing any drugs, for the last three months, if only because I had begun to doubt that I could. Without any outside chemicals, I was able to function and be happy, while I was here. That was an important thing for me to find out.

It doesn't mean I think I have totally solved my self-proclaimed problem, with drugs. I realize, my not doing drugs, while alone in the mountains, is not a true test of whether or not I will want to do them again, when I return, to the stresses, of normal life. I hope that I will not feel the need to find happiness, by smoking grass, or by dropping acid, in the future. And I am scared that I will.

My desire to see some winter wildlife was both rewarding and frustrating. Going into the woods, to be friends with the animals, just didn't seem to work out as well, as it did in all those family movies.

Being totally responsible for providing the wood to burn, to keep my cabin warm, has been a good growing experience for me. It has made my muscles grow. More importantly, heating with wood has increased my confidence, as a survivor.

Spending so much of my time here alone, has taught me to like myself more, as I had hoped it would, in the beginning of this book. I have come to the realization, each of us must be our own best friend, if we want to be able to be good friends to others. Through self-imposed isolation, I have learned that being alone is not the same as being lonely.

From talking about my past, aloud, into this recorder, I have heard the bitterness, in my voice, bitterness towards my parents, towards teachers, and bitterness towards a whole intangible system, which I felt let me down. I have also heard the sounds of hope, in my voice, hope for the future. One of the nicest things about recording this book, rather than just writing it, is being able to hear myself. As I got closer to the end, I noticed my voice sounded more hopeful, than it did bitter.

Establishing a close relationship with my dog, Misty, has fulfilled a boyhood fantasy of mine. Ever since I first saw the dog Lassie, on television, a series that ran from 1954 – 1973, I wanted a dog that wanted me. Somehow, the dogs I had as a child never worked out right. They always barked, when they weren't supposed to and they never seemed to do what I wanted. I've only had Misty for less than year, and already she knows, and obeys many commands, that I have taught her. Best of all, she likes and wants to be with me. I know, because I asked her.

Learning how to cook is not something I can credit to my Lime Kiln experience. I have always enjoyed cooking, but preparing each and every meal, for myself, was a new one.

The Yashica camera I bought on credit, before coming up here, has given me my first opportunity, at using a good thirty-five-millimeter. All the cameras I've had in the past were the just aim, shoot, and pray something comes out, variety. It has been a trip learning about F stops, and apertures, and such. Not sure how much I really learned.

Throughout my stay here, I have been learning and growing and experiencing. Whatever becomes of these twelve hours of tape recording, I know I will be better off, for having made them.

One other thing still troubles me though, as I prepare to leave today. I am troubled by the fact I set a goal for myself, of writing a book, which as of yet, still is not written. Even though I have done much work towards that goal, I still have not finished. Twelve hours of tape are just that, twelve hours of tape.

Twelve hours of tape do not a book make. There is still all

that typing someone must do and the editing. Oh God, the editing this mess of words will need, in order to make any sense, when someone tries to read it. All those run-on sentences will have to be chased down and stopped. The dangling participles can't be left dangling. Misplaced gerunds will have to be found and returned to their proper places. And the breaks in my speech, that might become excessive commas, could be a problem. You see, this sort of tell-it-as-you-go story book is a real nightmare for an editor.

Of course, I could just transcribe it exactly as I said it. Sort of a James Joyce style stream of unconsciousness – my own portrait of myself as a young man. Seriously though, my concern is that when I return to my carpentry business, back in Massachusetts, the goal of writing a book will never be realized. I am afraid I will have started another project I never finish, like so many others, from my past. I think I could deal with having written a book that nobody wants to read, because I would have, at least, accomplished something most people only talk about doing.

How many times have you heard somebody say they could write a book about what they know, but never do? To have talked about an entire book and never have written a word of it, so others could read what I've said, would leave me with an extreme sense of failure. This time, I would not be able to go to the mountains and write about my failures.

The answer then, for me, is to make sure I follow through and turn these tapes into a book, so you can read the words I have spoken. If you are reading this now, you know, I have done it.

EPILOGUE

December 25, 2022

Bringing you, my loyal readers, up to date.

Hello again. It has been exactly 44 years since I first spoke with you. Of course, it may not have taken you that long to read this far. Many things have gotten better for me, and some things have gotten worse for others. We now have another drug to say no to – Fentanyl.

In Memory of Glenn Foden

My best friend Glenn Foden, was one of the most supportive persons of my desire to free myself from drug use. He also was, extremely encouraging during my pursuits at becoming a published author.

I thank Rob Bluey and The Heritage Foundation for the free use of this thumbs up photo of Glenn and for his Ronald Regan cartoon at the end of this memorial. The cartoon was one of Glenn's last for The Daily Signal.

Early October, 1981

A little over a year had passed since returning from my drug-free zone in the mountains. More importantly to most New Englanders, the Boston Celtics won the NBA title that year. The new season would be starting at the end of the month and there were basketballs being dribbled between legs and shot into the air at most all of the school playgrounds. I was looking for new friends – non-using friends. Basketball courts seemed like a good place to find them.

When a game I was watching at the local neighborhood court in Chelmsford ended, one of the players walked over to me. He reached out his hand, and from beneath an unkempt beard he revealed the most genuinely disarming and completely welcoming smile I had ever seen from a man in my relatively short life by then, and has not yet been surpassed since. "Hi – Glenn Foden," he introduced himself.

I responded in kind, but with a much less intoxicating smile, "Richie," I called myself. That was strange as I had never used that as a nickname for myself and I'd never been called that by others. The name stuck. With my soon to be new basketball buddies I'd be Richie forevermore.

At 6 foot 3 and 235 pounds Glenn was a big lad – 3 inches taller and 50 pounds heavier than I. From having watched him rebound the ball I could tell his weight was mostly comprised of muscle and bone. His handshake confirmed this; however, it wasn't overly forceful as some first handshakes tend to be with men. Glenn had nothing to prove.

Very quickly Glenn and I became friends, but unlike other rapid-fire friendships of mine, ours lasted a lifetime. Politically we were polar opposite – me, the conscientious objector – die-hard-hippie – former drug user, and Glenn with a republican's conservative disposition – who never even smoked pot.

After basketball games, we often sat for hours in his vehicle or mine and discussed our differing world views. We expressed ourselves passionately but always with civility and never in a personally judgmental manner. Glenn became my role model for how to be a man, how to treat women and how to just be a good human being. Right now, I wish there were more men like Glenn in this country to help keep our civil and political discourse positive.

As Glenn was practicing his cartooning craft and looking for full-time work in his field, I remember him glibly telling me, "Richie, I read the obituaries first thing every day to see if any prominent cartoonists have died – and then I read the rest of the news to figure out what I want to satirize that day. You never know – my ticket to success might just be one death away."

For me Glenn was already successful. He was a success in how he treated others, particularly strangers, and in how he valued friendships. In 1986, he'd find further success at a newspaper in Maryland, and after meeting Teresa at that same paper, as a faithful husband and a devoted father of twins.

In the interim, while I was restarting my carpentry business, I hired Glenn, part-time. His work ethic was great and what he lacked in carpentry skills, which was mostly everything, he made up for by his sunny disposition and uplifting spirit on construction sites. Being damn strong didn't hurt either.

Outside of work and basketball, Glenn orchestrated summertime trips for us, and our mutual basketball friends. Camping at Baxter State Park in Maine was our most common destination. From there we would go whitewater rafting during the day, and play cards in our portable screen house at night. We played for peanuts; literally.

Most nights, after staying up until morning, Glenn and I were the last to crawl back into our separate tents. Sometimes moose would wander through our campsite and delay our getting to sleep even longer. Once, upon encountering two of those impressive animals, a cow and calf, Glenn whispered, "Richie aren't they amazing and we get to be with them for free." My friend always had an appreciation for simple, inexpensive, and natural pleasures – no drugs needed.

Sometimes, we played our own version of picture charades. If Glenn was on your team you were likely to win. His abilities as a cartoonist allowed him to express most anything in as little as three lines. And, although he eventually made a fulltime

Staying Stoned

living in the cartoon industry, including a stint at the Los Angeles Times, I think you will agree, the sketches he made for me in this book are not cartoon like – they are artfully drawn.

Glenn had some great guiding principles for life. One of those principals was his willingness to do anything for a friend with no payback expected, as long as it didn't pertain to his marketable artistic skills. If you needed his help to move furniture or rake leaves – you could count on him. Need art and you'd have to pay. When I told him about *Staying Stoned* and asked him if he'd go back to Lime Kiln campground with me to make some sketches, he replied yes with enthusiasm. He also made an exception to his rule by not charging me on completion of his pen and ink drawings. He told me he was willing to wait until the book was published. Poor Glenn is still waiting.

After Glenn married and became a father our excursions to the backwoods of Maine and the mountains of New Hampshire were replaced by summer visits on my back porch or at Glenn's parents' house. Other than that, Glenn and I stayed in touch by phone, not weekly or even monthly, sometimes only yearly. But always on Groundhogs' Day – Glenn's birthday – an easy date to remember – no Facebook reminders required. And whenever we did speak, other than catching up about the events in our lives, it always felt like time had stood still for us. Our relationship remained solid.

So, even though *Staying Stoned* still hadn't gotten published yet, and Glenn's sketches sat in a box in my closet, when I asked him to draw the cover for my second book, *Saving Papa's Tales*, he was willing and able.

On Friday, March 18, 2016, at 6:22 a.m. EST, I received the following text from him: "Hey Richie! Sitting in the airport waiting to head north... I'll give you a shout for coffee and maybe a donut or two...cu soon." This was Glenn's way of setting up a business meeting.

A day passed without my hearing a "shout" from him. When I called his cell phone there was no response. The weekend passed. On that Monday, I decided to call his dad's house in Chelmsford where I knew he was staying. "Hi, Donald – it's Richie. I understand your *Sunny* boy is up visiting with you."

"Glenn is gone, Richie," he offered no more than that at first.

I questioned him further, "Is everything all right in Maryland? Did he have to go back early?"

"No, Richie – Glenn died last night," Donald told me, and then started sobbing before hanging up.

It was the worst of times for me and anyone who knew Glenn. Even those that only met him once or twice were saddened. He had that rare impact on people. I am grateful for the hours I had alone with Glenn and I am pleased we maintained our closeness for 35 years despite miles of separation for many of those years. At 60, a prominent cartoonist died; that cartoonist was Glenn Foden. There was no satire on that day.

Obviously, Staying Stoned the recording has been turned into the printed word, and Glenn's sketches are finally gracing the pages of this book. But it wasn't easy.

Turning recordings into the printed word

I spent approximately two years transcribing those tapes. Playing back the recorded words, one or two sentences at a time, I used an electric typewriter, and many hand scribbled notes to put it all on paper. Remember, this predated the advances we now have in this digital world – no personal computers capable of turning magnetic tape recordings into printed words, and no internet.

When I finished that slow, arduous task, I began looking for a publisher. None of the major publishing houses were interested, and the rejection letters piled up.

I decided to contact one of the "Just Say No" organizations that had popped up in California, thanks to Nancy Regan. I spoke on the phone with a representative and told them about my book. They seemed interested and invited me to come see them. So, in 1982, I flew to California at my own expense, and handed them, in person, a very rough copy of my manuscript. After reading it, they just said, "No." The words, photos, and sketches got put away in a closet and were not revisited for 33 years.

Acknowledgment

Then in 2015, I met Doctor Gregory LaBranche, a PhD in psychology and the founder of Virtu Services Network, an addiction recovery service. We became friends.

Doc, as I called him, was not a sit behind his desk kind of therapist. He spent most of his time on the streets helping to keep his clients' safe. Harm reduction was his number one goal in treating those with addictions – any kind of addictions.

When I told him about my three months in the mountains

getting sober, he was intrigued. He asked to read the manuscript. And that is how *Staying Stoned* came out of the closet.

Christmas Day, 2022
Some final thoughts

When you, or someone you care about is struggling with addiction, harm reduction is key. If you have tried some forms of therapy, but none seemed to work, keep trying. Remember, there is no one solution that works for everyone. And most of us, myself included, can't just simply, say no. There is help out there – nonjudgmental help! You needn't climb a snow-covered mountain to find it.

Thanks for spending time with me,
Richard T. Ebner   aka: Theo or Richie

I have listed some resources for addiction recovery services at my website, and I will update them as time goes on.

richardebner.com

Richard Ebner